BALLET TO THE CORPS

A MEMOIR

by Marie Paquet-Nesson

For my parents
Marie and Philip Paquet

and
Robert Joffrey and Gerald Arpino

With deep gratitude for my husband, Jero Nesson, and his invaluable help.

Thanks to Debra Cash for her suggestions, Ann Haddad for her early encouragement, and Debra Maher for her expertise.

Thanks also to Dianne Consoer Leech, Ellen Everett Kimiatek, and Suzanne Hammons Daone.

Cover design: Paul Maher
Book design and editing: Debra Maher

CONTENTS

ILLUSTRATIONS

Chapter 1

GETTING OFF THE GROUND

The 1955 Boston Arts Festival ballet performance fell on the same evening as my high school graduation ceremony. My joy at having completed high school was now matched by not having to attend the ceremony.

I had slogged through each school day, year after year, until the afternoon bell set me free. Free to tear out the building and down the street, catch a trolley and transfer to the elevated train, and arrive (an hour later) in downtown Boston at my ballet school to be with my friends. And now, I was excused from attending a long ceremony at a school for which I cared nothing, with black-capped and gowned students with whom I had little in common. I was giddy with my good fortune.

My costume, a short, peach-colored Grecian style tunic, not a cap and gown, represented and foretold—I was sure—my future. For months we had been rehearsing "Spring," "Summer," "Fall," and "Winter" sections from Vivaldi's score, *The Seasons*. We wanted our ballet teacher, Alicia Langford, to be proud of us.

She and her new husband, Edwin Binney, were intent on having The Alicia Langford School of Ballet considered a professional school. Having fallen in love with both ballet and Miss Langford, Edwin Binney, a magna cum laude Harvard graduate student, used his pedigree and public relations savvy to work towards that end.

Our annual recitals were now called concerts. Concerts sounded grand, whereas recitals connoted a steady stream of tutued children toe and tapping through hours of routines. Miss Langford's girls wanted to live up to the concert designation.

It is not uncommon for young teenage girls to have crushes on their female dancing schoolteachers and we adored beautiful Miss Langford. She had danced professionally just long enough to have had garnered several excellent reviews and to have had her picture taken with Sol Hurok, the preeminent impresario of the day. We acolytes were sure that her career, foreshortened by marriage and children,

The author at age 15 taking class at Alicia Langford School of Ballet and her partner, "Joseph, the fisherman," 1952. (From the collection of Marie Paquet-Nesson)

was the undoubted reason for her melancholy smile. Or maybe it was the divorce from her first husband. She was the only divorced person any of us knew personally. As a divorcée, our beloved teacher was not only beautiful, but mysterious as well.

We liked Edwin well enough. Any reservations we may have had about him vanished with his choreographic and partnering ability. He also arranged for performances at the Boston Arts Festival and, more memorably, another at The Isabella Stewart Gardner Museum, which meant that we danced for audiences of "real" people (not primarily parents, aunts, uncles, siblings, and reluctant cousins). Partly on the strength of those performances and, in particular, the one at the magical Gardner Museum, three of my friends and I were spurred on in our quest to become ballerinas.

We performed in the Tapestry Room—also referred to as the Music Room— of the fifteenth century Venetian-inspired palace. Located in the Fenway area of Boston, Mrs. Gardner opened her museum on New Year's night, 1903. It was built to her personal specifications for the expressed purpose of displaying her impressive art collection. Captivating all who enter, it is the courtyard that seduces the senses away from daily life. Fragrant flowers and lush plants border a second century Roman tiled floor. Three stories of Venetian, stone-arched windows rise above and a glass roof emits light and warmth.

Our dressing room was a small ground floor gallery. There were four of us, each in identical mid-length white costumes made of tarlatan (a stiffened cheesecloth material) and crowns of pink and blue flowers. (Nylon netting was not yet commonly used.) I was the last to finish dressing. Alone, I began walking along the broad corridor. I could hear water splashing from the far end of the courtyard. Moonlight poured over the ancient Medusa mosaic in the center of the tiled floor. Wearing shiny pink pointe shoes, I carefully rolled through my toes onto the balls of my feet and stepped down into the courtyard. I ignored the Keep Off sign and took one tiny, deliberate step after another. Moonlight pulled me across time and distance. In the Music Room, my place was waiting for me.

It seemed as if the ballet was over in a few fleeting moments. We young dancers had danced well. Back in our dressing room, we changed out of our costumes and took off our make-up. Congratulating one another, we happily tumbled over each other's words as we hurried past the courtyard and back up the stairs, this time to the Dutch Room, a room where Mrs. Gardner had given dinner parties. There was a long table in the center of the room that had been set with china, silver, and servings of Lobster Newburg for approximately twenty people. The dancers and my mother—who had volunteered to help with the costumes—had been invited to join what I assumed to be a select group from the audience.

Facing us was a wall hung with two large Rembrandt paintings. The double portrait of a middle-aged, merchant class couple (dressed in black and white with minutely detailed lace neck ruffs) looked austerely over us. The other painting, Christ and his (very frightened) disciples in a boat being tossed by a stormy sea, seemed not to look at us but to draw us in. "Turn around," my mother said to us. Just above our heads was the artist himself as a young man in a small self-portrait.

(As an adult and frequent visitor to the museum, I grew very fond of the two large Rembrandts. They, along with a sublime Vermeer and ten other priceless works, were stolen in the great 1990 art heist. Many Bostonians and art lovers everywhere, feel as though they have been robbed of a piece of their personal history. I am one.)

The next day our lives were back to familiar concerns and obsessions. Having a good class to gain Miss Langford's approval was the most important hour and a half of the day. Maybe because there was parity among us in talent and achievement, our friendships were knitted closely through mutual ambition and insecurity. We also practiced and coached one another after classes and on Sundays and during school vacation days.

Laurie and I were neighbors and particular friends, and we practiced diligently together. We practiced on my family's cement basement floor where we suffered through the occasional shin split and, less frequently, in her family's either too cold or too hot attic. "Ye Gad Zooks," "For the love of Mike," and much more daringly, "Darn," we would exclaim in frustration as we struggled to jump higher, turn more revolutions, and stretch our limbs. We sat on each other's pointed feet in the hopes of higher insteps. We grabbed each other's legs and forcibly yanked them, rather brutally as I remember, as high as our strength would allow. And we pushed one another into normal and sideways splits with equally ruthless determination.

After an hour and a half of more painful than instructive work, we indulged ourselves by taking turns being the Swan Queen and Giselle. What fun that was! With an Eugene Ormandy recording of the great Tchaikovsky *Swan Lake* score playing as loudly as the record player would allow and lovingly partnered by well placed high backed chairs, we reenacted the romantic pas de deux. Even more emotionally satisfying, we danced and acted the mad scene from *Giselle*. Jilted by a handsome prince who had misled Giselle into believing that he was a simple peasant boy and in love with her, the gentle, innocent Giselle goes mad. The scene that follows is one of the dramatic scenes that a true ballerina conquers. Laurie and I were sure that our portrayals portended our futures.

As young ballet students, we all were preoccupied with our bottoms. Were they too big? Ed Binney admonished us for having American "behinds," "They should be out of sight," he said, "think of the British word 'bottoms.'" To that end, we bought rubber pants. Sold in drug stores for infants and toddlers, these were paper-thin, rubber pants meant to be worn over cloth diapers. Of course, they fit loosely over babies' bottoms. On us, they were skin snug and unseen under tights and leotards. Miss Langford had wanted us to wear some kind of tummy binder. (Female dance belts were sold for the purpose.) It is important to keep your insides in place, she had explained, so that we would not risk our ability to have children. This did not seem like an important consideration, but the rubber pants fit the bill. They not only protected our future chances at motherhood, but they made us sweat like football players. The sweat, we believed, reduced our behinds to smaller bottoms.

One of our hobbies was collecting dance pictures in newspapers or magazines. They were few but find them we did, and every one was pasted into scrapbooks. We collected baseball card size photographs of famous dancers that Capezio dance supply stores gave away. We examined each face, costume, and perfect pose over and over. With each purchase of shoes and tights, our collection grew. We did not trade them, just collected them. We took special note of the signatures that seemed to dance across the edge of the photo. Each one had loops and curlicues. We began practicing our own signatures. Some of us toyed with changing our names and others added a French accent ague or grave to theirs. When the day came—and surely it would—when someone would ask us for an autograph, we would be ready.

Saturdays were special. After class we put off our long trolley rides home. Squeezing into a booth at Brigham's ice cream shop, a half dozen of us lingered over hot fudge sundaes. We talked through the entire class, bemoaned every fallen turn, and in turn, commiserated and bolstered each other's spirits.

A second topic of interest was the men in our class. They were all basically beginning students but, men being in very short supply in the 1950s, they were placed into advanced classes and partnering classes almost as soon as they walked through the door. Ed Binney was in our advanced class along with three other college men. There was a fifth man, Joseph, whose job as a commercial fisherman kept him from attending classes regularly. When he did show up, he usually smelled of liquor. He was a sweet fellow but none of us wanted to get too close to the mingled scents of fish and tavern. Neither do I remember any of us having a crush on any of the men. We did wonder if any of them were "queer" or were "fairies," words we did not use with any particular negative connotation. They were just the words we knew. As far as I know, none of us had any clear idea as to how "they" "did it." I, for one, had absolutely no idea. It never occurred to us to ask our mothers.

Now, early summer 1955, all of us had finished our senior year in high school. The Boston Arts Festival concert was over and classes with Miss Langford were coming to an end. A few of my friends were nervous about taking the next step: moving to New York City for further study and taking auditions. I reminded them of the previous summer we had spent together in New York and how we had thought that a table at Horn and Hardardt Automat would be a suitable substitute for the booth at Brighams. We reminisced about New York studios and we laughed about our discovery that in New York not only did no one wear rubber pants, but also all the bottoms and behinds were pretty much equal in size.

Chapter 2

NEW YORK CITY

I had little nostalgia about leaving my family and Miss Langford or Boston and Brighams. The security of having had Laurie, my chum (as we special friends referred to one another), precede me, and the knowledge that my family would lovingly welcome me back, allowed me to indulge in fearless optimism. I also had the experience of three previous visits to New York. Without each of them I would, most likely, not have been a dancer.

My first visit to New York was when I eight years old. My parents put me on the train, asked the conductor to look after me, and told me that they were proud of their big girl. I was met at New York's Grand Central Station by my aunt and uncle.

They took me to Radio City Music Hall. Enthralled, I sat forward in my seat. On the vast, distant stage there were lights, music, and dancers. Hundreds of dancers in gauzy, white skirts floated through the air. I was in fairyland. In that moment I knew that I belonged among those magical creatures. I would be a dancer, and from that moment it never occurred to me that I would not.

I prepared a performance for my parents upon my return home. I put on my party dress and new, black patent leather shoes, rubbing them with a thin film of Vaseline so that they shone. "Close your eyes," I commanded my parents. The family record player was in the corner of the living room. Carefully, I put the needle down on a 78-rpm recording of a Strauss Waltz. "Now, open your eyes," I said and began to dance. I was back in the enchanted land of Radio City Music Hall and in this enchanted land I remained, through the last rather tinny chords of the recording. My parents clapped and clapped. Two weeks later they sent me to dancing school where I traded my black patent leather shoes for pink ballet slippers.

After only four months of once-a-week classes, I was thrilled to be told that I was ready for toe shoes. This was a milestone that I had anticipated with impatience. My class of knobby-kneed eight- and nine-year olds was fitted with Dura Toes (clunky, leather-tipped toe shoes). At the steep price of three dollars per pair, mothers were happy to be assured that the shoes would last through and beyond their girls' next growth spurt. "Perch point, perch point," we heard as we struggled to rise and balance on weak legs and ankles. Dura Toes were well suited for preventing little feet from collapsing forward over the shoes, but they had no effect in assisting our efforts to actually get up onto our toes.

In 1945 most dance schools taught toe, tap, ballet, baton twirling, and, in South Boston, Irish step dancing. Fortunately, my mother, who had a heart for the arts though no experience in any of them, loved books. She discovered that my classes did not resemble the careful descriptions and drawings in her most recent library acquisition, *The Classical Ballet Primer*. And "perch point" did not show up in the book's glossary.

My mother wrote to the Ballet Russe de Monte Carlo—the best-known American company at the time—and asked for the name of a classical ballet teacher in Boston. The company wrote back with one name, Alicia Langford. After three additional years of decidedly more competent instruction, I won my toe shoes back. They were not iron-like Dura Toes, but the more pliant Pavlovas. These, and the two thousand additional toe shoes I would ultimately use, were referred to, alternatively and more professionally, as "pointe shoes."

The second time I arrived at New York's Grand Central Station I was with my family. I was fifteen and had been taking ballet classes for seven years. My mother took me uptown to the School of American Ballet while my father, brother, and sister went to the Statue of Liberty.

SAB, as it is familiarly called, is the official school of the New York City Ballet, George Balanchine's company. Now, as well as then, mothers with daughters in tow were looked on with suspicion at best and with certain distain if they presented their children as "exceptional" and "deserving of special treatment." This was an elite school and students were accepted by audition only. Neither class level nor numbers of classes to be taken were negotiable. If SAB said you were not accepted, you were not. If SAB said your proficiency was fit for level B, level B it was. If SAB said there were seven level B classes per week, you took seven, not six and not eight. And no one asked to take a single class, let alone a single class in the advanced division.

My mother, however, was determined to find out if her fifteen-year old daughter had a reasonable chance of fulfilling her dream of being a professional dancer. She wanted an evaluation from one of SAB's teachers and my mother was going to make that happen. Madame Eugenie Ouroussow, an imposing Russian lady and the school's executive director, sat just off the entryway. She was not a large woman, but her demeanor dwarfed the desk and all those who approached her. "Get dressed," my mother instructed me.

The dressing room was crowded with SAB students. I put on my royal blue tunic, a far cry from SAB's regulation black leotard, but the current fashion at my Boston ballet school. Looking in the mirror, I licked my fingers and wet down my hair. Nervous, my face was flushed a brilliant pink against the royal blue. I went back out to the desk and a stern Madame Ouroussow. My mother appeared to be pleading. Neither she nor I knew that the austere man seated next to Madame Ouroussow was the advanced class teacher, Anatole Ouboukof, a Russian compatriot of Mr. Balanchine's. After eyeing me as I walked toward the desk, he gave a terse nod and I was allowed to take the class. What I did not know was that I was allowed to take the class only on the condition that I would leave if Mr. Ouboukof said I was not advanced enough.

So that is how I happened to be at the barre, standing in first position in Mr. Ouboukof's advanced class. From reputation, I knew that his difficult classes and stern personality terrified many students. The official advanced students and I took our places at the barre and waited for class to begin. Generally, a teacher enters and gives the first exercise followed by general corrections. Some teachers give individualized corrections as they walk by their students. Mr. Ouboukof, I was startled to find out, singled out one student for corrections.

On this day, he chose me. Standing directly in front of me, he looked like a retired discus thrower who hadn't lost any of his bulky strength. His fingers snapped sharply two inches in front of my face and they followed me, "snap, snap, snap," as my knees bent in the first plié. "And one!" he roared before each phrase. He spoke with a strong accent. "Ee won," he continued over and over. I took a deep breath. Lifting my head high, I rose above my fear. I danced better than I had ever danced before. My very life, I felt, depended on it. Mr. Ouboukof placed me in the first group and gave me corrections, a sure sign that a teacher likes you. I found myself doing steps I had never seen before. It didn't matter how badly I thought I might be executing them. I did not dare stop or falter. I kept going.

My mother waited on the other side of the door, knowing that each minute that passed without my coming through it was a good minute. After an hour and a half, the class ended and I left along with the rest of the students. My mother did not ask for an evaluation. I had not been thrown out of class and that was evaluation enough.

My third visit, spurred on by Miss Langford, was with three of my ballet friends. We were sixteen and seventeen years old and juniors in high school.

Every summer, hundreds of fervently dedicated ballet students descended on the studios of New York City. Eager to take ballet classes with the city's many excellent teachers, they also looked forward, if with some hesitancy, to see how well they fared alongside one another. Did they dance as well? Worse? Better? How old were the dancers who were better? Were they younger or older? Were they tall or short and how thin and how flexible? Would the young, out-of-town dancers have their resolve strengthened or diverted away from careers they had been working towards since they were young children? Seeing the competition, many students left their New York summers realizing that a professional career was out of reach. Others, even talented ones, chose not to continue, deciding that high school football games, record hops, and boys were more important than ballet.

Not so us. It did not matter that Manhattan was oppressively hot and the studios had neither air conditioning nor showers. It didn't matter that classes were so crowded that the teachers rarely asked for your name and, if they did, rarely remembered it. Being on our own was intoxicating and taking two and three classes a day with a variety of teachers was heaven on earth. We happily shared our unwavering commitment and, for six weeks, a hotel room. One bed and four rollaway cots patch worked across the floor. We walked on top of and over the never made rollaways to reach the bathroom. The city was always light and awake and we took evening walks. We ate all our meals at the Horn and Hardardt Automat on West 57th Street. The 1937 building—which unfortunately, was razed in late 2006—had a deco grandeur that satisfied our cosmopolitan pretensions and the food was cheap.

New York Automats were a cross between cafeterias and long, low vending machines turned on their sides. Waist high along the sides of the room were rows of little glass doors. Behind them were sandwiches, entrees, and desserts of Jell-O, cheesecake, rice pudding, and fruit. Inserting the required coins (a quarter for a hamburger and a nickel for a small glass of milk), the catches on the little doors released and the doors swung outward. Peering inside, I could see the lower half of people dressed in sanitary white as they scurried about, replacing what had just been bought.

Morning, noon, and night the restaurant was always busy, but never so crowded that we could not find a table. Sometimes we found ourselves sitting near an old woman dunking a used tea bag that she had pulled out of her shabby pocket book. The cup of hot water was free and, if lucky, she would have found an un-cleared table with a partially eaten meal left behind. How could this be, we wondered. Didn't she have a kitchen? Each of us began leaving food on our plates. Homelessness was an alien concept to us.

After the evening meals we discussed the classes of the day and lamented a missed pirouette or rejoiced in a teacher's encouraging word. There would be no happier summer than this one.

Ultimately, only three of us would move to New York. We remained friends and found new ones.

Chapter 3

SEEKING MY FORTUNE

I never doubted that I would become a professional and neither, apparently, did my parents. The day had come. It was time for me to leave home. For the occasion they gave me their large cowhide suitcase—once their honeymoon luggage—one-hundred dollars in cash from a matured ten-dollar savings bond, and their confidence in my success. On this long planned-for day they drove me to the New York New Haven Railroad station in suburban Boston. Waiting by a wooden shelter with my parents were my thirteen-year old brother and nine-year old sister. They hung back and were unusually quiet. They had watched the progress towards my departure for most of their lives. I chatted happily with my mother who never became a "ballet mother" but had, over the years, made wise decisions for me. More important, she tempered her enthusiasm, always matching it to my commitment. The choice to dance was my own. My father deferred to my mother's greater artistic knowledge.

The train chugged noisily into view. The coal-fueled engine swirled noxious fumes around us as we kissed goodbye. I climbed the steep steps of the rail car and my dad lifted the suitcase and set it beside me. I was wearing a circular skirt: blue, mid-calf length, freshly starched, and ironed. My high-heeled shoes were new and they had pointed toes. My brown and white saddle shoes were packed in my suitcase but I knew that I would throw them out as soon as I arrived in New York. I waved from my seat and watched my family begin to recede.

At seventeen and a half years, my life was my own. I went to the dining car where the tables had stiff, white, linen tablecloths and little anchored-down, silver-plated bud vases. Each vase had one red rose. I was completely at home and carefree. Rattling through the dark, long tunnel into Grand Central Station felt significantly different than previous times. On this day, the tunnel represented a passage from not being a New Yorker to becoming a New Yorker.

The YWCA was a first lodging for many young women arriving in New York. Safe and inexpensive, I lived there until I took over a furnished room from a friend.

Her, and now my, third floor room—along with many other brownstone rooms—had a window overlooking a common courtyard with straggly trees and rusted garden chairs. It was hot. All windows were open. Three weeks into my new life my mother came to visit. Sharing the double bed, I felt protective of my forty-three year old mother. "Don't worry," I said to her, as the nightly obscenities began to reverberate throughout the courtyard.

The next day she moved me into a larger furnished room on a different street in the West Sixties. I would be living with Laurie, my chum from Boston, and her roommate. Two years older than I, Laurie had moved to New York the year before. Her large studio apartment had once been the brownstone's parlor, its elegance long gone. The Victorian plaster moldings and ceilings needed paint but the gilt framed mirror was large enough for three primping ballerina-bound hopefuls. An old stove and refrigerator were set against one wall near the bathroom. The sink served functions of both bath and kitchen. Waist length strands of hair and bits of food clogged the drain. Washed leotards, tights, and bras drip-dried from every doorknob, chair, and bureau edge.

Laurie had a good Roman Catholic head on her shoulders. My mother thought she would have a good influence on me. I accompanied her to St. Patrick's Cathedral on Sunday mornings and, every now and then, to confession on Saturday afternoons.

It was Laurie who saved the soul of another of our Boston friends. Joan, a newly employed Rockette at Radio City Music Hall, called on us one evening. Tearfully, she told us that she had sinned with one of the stagehands in a utility closet. "With mops and brooms?" I asked incredulously. "And it happened more than once?" I was even more incredulous. "What will happen if you die tonight?" Laurie demanded of tearful Joan. A mortal sin—as hers surely was—not confessed would doom the sinner to eternal hell, or so we believed in 1955.

So, at ten o'clock on a Saturday night Laurie and I escorted Joan to the local Catholic Church. We rang the emergency bell. The door opened and a young priest appeared. I took several quick steps aside as Laurie pointed to Joan and said, "She needs to go to confession." We trooped behind the priest into the church. Laurie and I sat in a pew while Joan disappeared into the confessional, a mahogany closet-like structure with two doors. The priest went into one and closed the door. Joan went into the other and closed the door. I knew the procedure. With a light scraping sound, the wood shuttered window would have opened and Joan would be face to ear with the priest.

After five minutes Joan emerged and, out of respect, I didn't look at her until she had reached the altar to pray. Joan's immaculate soul restored, we left and headed directly to our neighborhood coffee shop for a hot chocolate.

I determined that I would never be similarly distracted from my dancing goals.

My next step was to get a job dancing, a job that required a union card. Within two weeks I had one.

Chapter 4

AUDITIONS

I began to take two and three classes a day. Scrutinizing my competition, I decided that I needed an additional year of study to be good enough for a major ballet company. Classes, however, were expensive. It became apparent that a frugal diet of cereal, frankfurters, and yogurt was not going to stretch out my hundred dollars for long. Dancers who could prove that they were professional by producing a union card qualified for greatly discounted rates. Any professional dancing job, even one of short duration, would do.

Professional dancers lent prestige, I presumed, and drew the much higher paying nonprofessional students to dance schools all over Manhattan. I not only longed not to be among the amateur ranks, but I was desperate to avoid the use of my despised high school typing course.

Dressing rooms were reliable places to hear about auditions for companies large and small, ballet and modern; as well as for shows for Broadway, off Broadway, summer stock, industrial shows, and nightclubs. I learned that Radio City Music Hall Ballet Corps was holding auditions. Summer replacements were needed, a perfect opportunity for acquiring a union card.

Dancers in the Radio City's Rockettes and Ballet Corps were two separate dance troupes until 1972 when the ballet was disbanded. They performed four or five shows a day, seven days a week for three consecutive weeks. The fourth week was off. Additionally, every summer extra dancers were hired. I took and easily passed the audition for the ballet corps. In two days time, I had a costume fitting and had begun rehearsing.

The rehearsal studio was the size of the stage and the floors of both were marked with assigned numbers; mine was twenty-three. Locating our places on stage easily and quickly was essential. Lines of dancers in rows and diagonals, straight and zigzagged, as well as patterns in the tableaux (a well-used Radio City choreographic tool) demanded that each spot be filled accurately, as well as gracefully. The actual execution of steps—or so it seemed to me—was secondary in importance.

A bevy of Rockettes and ballet dancers were rotated on turntables or raised up and down on elevated platforms. We moved and danced forward, back, left, and right. Performing with smiles and sequins to the Strauss *Emperor Waltz* eighty-four times in three weeks was not the peak experience I had imagined it would be those long nine years ago. It didn't matter. I was earning $80 per week and I held an AGVA (American Guild of Variety Artists) card. I was a professional. When my three weeks were over, I would be able to take as many classes as my heart desired and my energy level allowed.

Along with taking classes dancers took as many auditions as possible, not only for potential jobs but also for honing essential auditioning skills. "Picking up" combinations quickly, reproducing them accurately, and performing them with a unique quality increased chances of success.

Auditions were held in midtown dance studios or on the stages of currently running Broadway shows. Whether it was dancing for men and women seated in neat lines of chairs against studio mirrors or in the first rows of dimly lit theaters, auditioning was an intimidating experience. In a studio, we were accustomed to mirror checks for technical points, not staring into the eyes of our judges. In a theater the light was neither bright enough on stage nor dark enough in the "house" to create a barrier between the featureless faces and us.

Men and women, or boys and girls as we were then called, auditioned separately. There were always many more women than men. We positioned ourselves in groups of twenty. The first "cut" was determined by size and body type. We usually had an accurate idea of what type of dancer was needed going into an audition, but occasionally we were wrong so we were watchful. Hopefully, we wouldn't hear our first "thank you" before we had a chance to dance. "Thank you" really meant "no thank you." "Thank yous" came after each dance combination until, if we were lucky, we might hear the sweet words, "Come back to the finals." A rejection, even if we had no interest in the job, would make picking through the stacked dance bags a painfully self-conscious experience and an interminably long leave-taking. Piled in corners or under backstage prop tables, the assorted dancers' bags rose to the heights of mini mountains. The earlier in the audition we were excused, the deeper the mountain in which to plow for one's own bag and the keener the sense of failure.

Getting close to "making an audition," was cause for rejoicing. I was elated when I came close to replacing one of two dancers in a Lerner musical, *Plain and Fancy*. The romanticized Amish-theme production had run long enough for some of the original dancers to have moved on to other shows. One replacement was needed for a sophisticated, worldly type—the fancy in *Plain and Fancy*. A second opening was for a homebody type—the plain part, and the one for which I was auditioning. My great personal triumph was executing a two-minute jazz improvisation. Not having taken a jazz class in my life did not deter me. Undaunted, I picked up movements from the dancers who proceeded me. I threw myself onto the stage and danced my jazzy heart out. I survived to continue the audition. Although I did not get the job, I lasted until the end. When I finally did hear "thank you," it was a personal look-in-the-eye "thank you," not a big blanket dismissal tossed to a whole group.

I took only one industrial show audition. It was for an auto show featuring the introduction of the "must-have" Chevrolets. Dancers were being hired to twirl and kick around the oversized pink and turquoise bodies; to gesture and caress gleaming fins and grilles; and to smile, beckon, and flirt with the auto dealers. The money and short-term work was appealing. I can do that, I thought. So I went to the Coliseum at Columbus Circle at 59th Street where the audition and, eventually, the show would be held. (The twentieth century New York master builder, Robert Moses, proclaimed the Coliseum—which looked more like a mausoleum—as the "Exposition Capital of the World." It is now the site of the twenty-first century Time Warner building.)

Entering the dressing room I saw many Marilyn Monroe and Jane Russell look-a-likes. They were real showgirls: women, really. They looked as though they had just stepped out of a movie set, certainly not a ballet class. After seeing one halter-top, exposed midriff after another, partially exposed buttocks and legs in black fish net stockings, and feet in impossibly high-heeled shoes, I knew I was in unfamiliar territory. Their hair was stiffened into the latest coiffure and their painted faces would have made Madame Revlon proud. I looked at my pink ballet tights, pink ballet slippers, and black leotard. I looked at my modestly curved and covered body and hurried into a bathroom stall. I took wads of toilet paper to fill out my size 32A bra. "Better," I assured myself, although not even close to the conical breasts in the adjoining room. I took my sunrise coral pink lipstick and applied it as thickly as I could. I removed the rubber band and barrette from my bun, deciding that cascading hair was at least marginally more suitable than the bun on the back of my head.

The audition was held in a large room with a piano, pianist, and a number of sleazy, sixty-something men with thinning, glossy hair. Before the first notes on the piano were struck, a dozen or so dancers were told that they were not right and could leave. Of course, I was one of them, looking the least appropriate among even the rejected. I felt like someone's little sister. Leaving the building, I turned right, walked to 57th Street, and took another class.

Before and after this class, and all other classes during the following week, Metropolitan Opera Ballet auditions were being discussed. I had no idea that opera included dance and opera companies might have their own ballet companies. The Metropolitan Opera Ballet would provide a steady job in New York City, allowing ample time for classes.

On the day of the audition, I decided to wear a red and white flowered tunic to help me stand out from the sea of more conservative, mostly black, colors. The audition consisted of a full class given by the choreographer, Zachary Solov. Scores of dancers squeezed together along the barres for the usual warm-up exercises. We had arrived early to give ourselves our own warm-up so that even during the barre work, each tiny nuance, as well as the most energetic movement, could be executed as meticulously or as grandly as possible. After the barre work, dancers whose bodies were deemed not proportioned well enough, as well as those whose barre work was not precise enough, were let go.

Elimination continued during the center work (combinations of steps done away from the barre and in the center of the room). After forty-five minutes of combinations, thirty happy dancers, I among them, heard, "Come back tomorrow."

Wanting to increase my chances of being remembered from the day before, I wore the same flowered tunic the next day. I was not nervous and danced with happy abandon. "Come back tomorrow," I heard again. We were fifteen dancers left. There were five places to be filled.

The third day's audition class was the most challenging. It ended with thirty-two fouettes. This stock-in-trade series of turns is done in place on one leg while the other helps with a whipping around motion. If, eventually, a dancer becomes a ballerina, she is expected to perform this feat in the "Black Swan Pas de Deux." Audiences wait for this bravura moment, silently counting each turn before breaking into applause at the flashy finish. Although it was unlikely that opera ballet choreography would include fouettes, requiring them in auditions was a convenient and time efficient way of weeding out less accomplished technicians. Even Radio City, where the chance of fouettes being incorporated into the choreography was extremely remote at best, the audition included sixteen of them.

We heard Zachary Solov say, "Thirty-two fouettes en pointe." Spinning our heads around (called spotting) with each turn, we began. My trick was to count backwards from thirty-two. By counting backwards the turns at the end of the series seemed easier. The numbers "3-2-1" were more energizing than "30-31-32." I was on fouette number twenty-four and counting down. I was getting dizzy. To prevent the room from whirring into one continuous ribbon of light, dancers spot even harder, forcing their eyes to rest for a millisecond at the front of the room. On each turn we lifted ourselves up onto our toes, turned, and then came down off our toes at each turn's end. Up turn down, up turn down, thirty-two times on the same foot. With eight more to go, the girl beside me began to reel. "Keep steady," I told myself. I was not going to let that wobbling top to my right make me falter. I would not be budged. "Before that happens," I promised myself, "my fouette leg will whack her in the stomach." Sweat was flying off our faces as we spun, the droplets catching the light. I kept counting, "8-7-6-5." The chords on the piano grew louder, "4-3-2-1" and it was over.

Wisely, my careening neighbor avoided possible injury and had finished early. The rest of us held the ending pose with arms and head lifted in serene triumph. We held it for a full five seconds as we had been taught. Holding that last pose is akin to the echo of the last notes in a piece of music. It allows the eye, ear, and mind to see and hear beyond the movement and sound.

The sweat was now pouring down our faces, burning our eyes and tasting salty on our tongues. We came out of our poses and stood there in silence. The choreographer and his assistant/ballet mistress were talking to each other. As we waited, we untied our toe shoe ribbons, readjusted our tights, and recaptured flyaway hair or began to undo our tied-up hair altogether. Just as we were running out of things to distract us the choreographer spoke. "We have your names," he said. "Someone will call you over the weekend." We left.

The following evening as I sat down with my favorite Swanson's fried chicken TV dinner, the phone rang. I jumped over to it, letting two rings go by. To hide my anxiety, I modulated my voice to a slow clear contralto. "Hello?" I said. A voice identified itself as being from the Metropolitan Opera. "We want to offer you a contract," it said; the details of the terms and salary and the where and when of signing blended together. "Yes, yes, thank you," I was saying. "Hurry up, hurry up," I was thinking. Finally, the conversation ended and I called my parents. "I made it. I made it!" I shouted into the phone. It was a mid 1950s, heavy, black telephone. Its long curled cord was solidly tethered to its base. As our conversation lingered over every detail, I pranced and twirled myself inside the cord and out again, a happy Maypole dance with Ma Bell. When, at last, we hung up, the phone rang again. "Marie," the voice said, "I'm so sorry but there's been a mistake. It is not you who is accepted. It is another Marie. We want you to come back for another audition." Dumb-founded, I stared into the phone. How could this happen? What does this mean? I slept fitfully.

Once again, I wore the red and white flowered tunic. However there would be no chance of getting lost in a crowd of dancers this time. We were only two and we both understood that one of us would be hired and the other would not. This last audition consisted of dance segments from opera ballets. There was an eighteenth century court dance, a tarantella, a Spanish dance, a segment reminiscent of Egyptian hieroglyphics, and a Belle Epoch can-can. Having had little experience with any style or step outside the classical repertory, I had no good idea of what I was doing. Memorizing sequences of unfamiliar steps took longer for me than many other dancers, but I knew that with rehearsals I would be able to tap, point, click, flex, and stamp my feet with precision and bend, twist, undulate, and sway my body with aplomb. And I always knew that I could bring to life qualities inherent in the choreography, whether they were flamboyant and strong or demure and delicate. Perhaps it was this ability that shone through.

My competitor, I thought, was rather old and unexceptional. I later learned that she was twenty-five and was previously known to the ballet mistress. The ballet mistress wanted her while the choreographer—the one with the ultimate power— wanted me. Months later I realized that the ballet mistress's favorite was, in fact, mature and competent and probably the perfect choice. I am grateful that the choreographer took a chance on me. I was far less finished, but held more promise and I had a beautiful face. In the end, we were both chosen. I now had two union cards: AGVA (American Guild of Variety Artists) covered nightclub performers and Radio City dancers and AGMA (American Guild of Musical Artists) covered classical dancers, musicians, and singers. I never used the AGVA card again, but the AGMA card saw me through the next thirteen years and two ballet companies.

Chapter 5

METROPOLITAN OPERA BALLET

Rehearsals began within a week. Turnover was generally not high but, as I remember, five new "ballet girls" and three "ballet boys" were hired for the 1955-56 season. The twenty-four women and twelve men in the Met Ballet represented just about every height, size, shape, and age as well as talent and professional experience that could be found in the city. Very tall and very short; rail thin and chunky; long limbed and long torsoed; teenaged (of which I was one of two), and close to forty—all worked together. Some dancers had a decade or more of professional experience and a few had little. Having come from a three-week stint at Radio City, I had the least experience and, at seventeen, I was the youngest. Before signing my contract, I needed a permission slip from either a parent or a guardian. Anyone twenty-one years old or older will do, I was told. I prevailed upon a twenty-one year old American Ballet Theatre dancer friend to be my parental stand-in. I did not want to bother my parents. After all, I was a professional ballet dancer and I would be considered an adult in New York State in a couple of months.

Metropolitan Opera dancers were attracted to the steady New York work and pay. Some dancers were married and a few had children. Others had been in ballet companies and were tired of traveling, but were not yet ready to retire. There were dancers who either did not have good enough bodies, talent, or technique to ever qualify for a major ballet company and there were dancers, such as myself, who had not given up on their lofty dreams and planned on an opera ballet stint of no more than a year or two before moving on. The variety of opera ballets from court dances to can-cans to classical pointe ballets was easily accommodated and even enhanced by the diversity of the dancers. There was, however, a common denominator. Even if we did not have spectacular ballet techniques, we had all had good training, assuring a professional finish to each opera ballet we presented.

The entire company took class together at nine thirty each morning and rehearsed until five thirty with an hour break for lunch. Beginning in late August and continuing until the fall season opened, we rehearsed Monday through Saturday,

The Metropolitan Opera. The author, in La Traviata, *1955. (From the collection of Marie Paquet-Nesson)*

after which we performed at night and rehearsed for upcoming operas during the day.

I loved going to the Metropolitan Opera House on 39th Street and Broadway. It had been built in 1854 and reminded me of the Boston Opera House on Huntington Avenue where, from the time I was eight years old, my mother took me to see the touring Ballet Russe de Monte Carlo and American Ballet Theatre. Both opera houses had velvet curtains, golden horseshoes, glittering opening nights, and inexpensive "standing room" spaces at the back of the orchestra level. It was the standees (opera and ballet's ardently devoted fans) that cheered those endless bravos, the sound of which reverberated, unforgettably, throughout my body. Bravos had to be earned, however. Every singer and dancer was closely critiqued and each was compared to his or her rival. Unrestrained adulation, as well as criticism, was reserved for the undisputed stars, prima donnas, and prima ballerinas.

The Boston Opera House, built in 1909, was demolished in 1957. The space, used as a parking lot until1972, is now the location of Speare Hall—a characterless Northeastern University building. The only clue to the area's former glory is a tiny side street, Opera Way. Passing by, I wonder if anyone notices and, if they do, does the curious street sign interrupt the speed of their steps or a halt to their thoughts?

The Boston Opera House had been doomed by The Boston Redevelopment Authority (BRA) and the trustees of Northeastern University. The opera house was declared structurally unsound, although it took three demolition companies to successfully destroy it. It was also said to have had poor acoustics. However, Wallace Sabine, a physics professor at Harvard and a member of the architectural team for the recently completed Boston Symphony Hall—considered to have one of the world's best acoustics—had been one of the opera house's acoustic consultants.

The demise of Boston's old opera house, spearheaded by forces outside the theater and music community, was starkly different than that of the old Met. It was the Metropolitan Opera itself that was eager to peel itself away from a less than prestigious location and a building that had been deemed too small for decades. The Metropolitan Opera Company was eager to relocate to the white marble cluster of theaters at Lincoln Center. Talk of plans for renovating the old house as well as pleas from Leonard Bernstein, Gian Carlo Menotti, Marian Anderson, and Leopold Stokowski, among others, was to no avail. Sadly, the old Met was demolished in 1967.

We used the "roof stage" as our dance studio at the old Met. Built over the stage area, it was the same size as the stage. Large paned, high windows let in lots of natural light. Two feet of horizontal radiators ran underneath. The walls were rough, unpainted brick. The ceiling was two stories high and there were no low hanging light fixtures for high-flying male dancers or lifted female dancers to dodge. This was impressive studio space. Low ceilings and pillars were common obstructions in the converted factory spaces often used by dance companies. (The New York Joffrey Ballet School's original Sixth Avenue location was a converted tie factory.) Dance companies combed Manhattan for additional and inexpensive rehearsal space. Bohemian Hall, located in an East Eighties Ukrainian neighborhood, was a popular choice; it had no weight-bearing pillars standing in the way. The hall, a function and clubroom in the evenings, was large and smelled faintly of beer. Stocky, Slavic men with florid faces sat at small, round tables in the adjoining restaurant and bar. They ceased speaking and looked up with indifference as we passed through on our way to rehearsal.

By contrast, the entrance to the Met dance studio was through the costume storage room. It had rows and rows of tall, narrow, wood closets. Each had hanger upon hanger of old costumes. Drab, muslin peasant dresses and breeches pressed close to scarves and wigs and headpieces of every imagination. Worn but still richly colored velvets were jammed against graying crinolines. The closets, floors, and walls were bone dry and were the color of bone. They smelled musty and stale. On our way to rehearsal, we felt close to the ghosts of the singers and dancers who had once breathed life into those costumes.

The day began with company class followed by a full company opera ballet. Dancers not being used in a particular segment rehearsed in small groups in the back corners of the studio being careful not to draw the attention of our choreographer, Zachary Solov. He needed to stay focused on the principal rehearsal, as did the rehearsal pianist.

Rehearsal pianists understood dancers' language. "Take it from the arabesque." "Take it from the sauté," they might have heard. Dancers and even choreographers were not always musically trained. Some had assistants to help them with difficult scores of Bartok or Ives. Some, like Balanchine, were excellent musicians and others just muddled along. Choreographers and dancers sometimes count differently than musicians, the movement rather than the musical score, being the guide. Rehearsal pianists were hard working and patient. They not only understood ballet technique, our particular phrasing and peculiar counting, but they played with color and energy, important qualities for demanding choreographers and weary dancers.

Rehearsals could be exhausting; muscles screaming after repeating unfamiliar passages over and over again. Numbing boredom often accompanied the exhaustion. During the years before stricter union rules were enforced, all of us were called for the full day. Sometimes long minutes, and even hours, passed before we were needed. Sitting against the wall under the barre with knees pulled up under our chins, we rested and gossiped. And we stretched. Lying on our backs, we pulled our legs over our heads. Seated, we extended our legs directly out from the hips in side splits. Then, chests pressed into the floor, we continued to rest and gossip during the long wait.

Except for popular Verdi and Puccini melodies, I knew nothing about opera, so I looked forward to the first rehearsal of each opera ballet. What would the triumphant march in *Aida* and the "monster" choreography in *Orpheus In The Underworld* be like? How many aristocratic balls would I grace, wearing a hooped gown, wig of curls, and heeled shoes? Dances in *Ernani*, *La Giaconda*, *La Perichole*, and *Die Fledermaus* were on pointe and it was these classical ballets to which I eagerly looked forward.

I was in many operas, including *Sampson and Delilah*. As a wispy adolescent, I was not assigned a partner for the *Sampson* orgy scene. Instead, another female dancer and I were placed in the back corners of the stage where we waved our arms and hoped we did not look too virginal. Nor was I a voluptuous dancer in *Carmen*, but was cast as a little boy in the little boy's chorus.

During the Met's regular season real little boys sang but on the six-week spring tour eight of us dancers took their places. Along with singing in French in *Carmen*, we sang an English version of *Boris Gudenov*, and in *Tosca* and *Il Travatore* we sang in Italian. Although, being an altar boy was fun, being an unruly street urchin and pushing, shoving, and jostling the Met chorus was even more fun. We smudged brown dirt-like makeup on our cheeks, pulled our jackets and caps askew, and practiced making brat-like faces. Last but not least, it was (and still is) amusing to watch the expressions of family and friends when they learned that I—who am known not to belt out even a musical *Happy Birthday*—sang with the New York Metropolitan Opera Company.

Before the start of the tour, we rehearsed with Maestro Walter Taussig. Rehearsing our untrained voices could not have been a prestigious assignment, but he was always a rather jolly fellow and following him to find some corner of the mezzanine lobby for rehearsal space was something of an adventure. We sat on little chairs borrowed from one of the nearby boxes.

Being in the little boys chorus had a prestige that being a "super" (supernumerary or extra) did not. Whenever an opera needed supers, the dancers were required to fill in. Our youth and agility added energy to street scenes and our grace lent authenticity to genteel parties. Although we received an additional three dollars for each performance, the money did not nearly compensate for a task we felt was way beneath our professional status. There would be exceptions, like being on stage with Renata Tebaldi in *La Traviata*, being in the third act of *Tales of Hoffmann*, and aerial swimming as one of Wagner's Rhine maidens.

During the 1955-56 season, the Met did a new production of *La Traviata* for the incomparable Renata Tebaldi. Karinska, the preeminent costumer, executed the costumes. A compatriot of Balanchine and for whom she would later design as well as make costumes had a career that spanned film and stage as well as opera and ballet. Born in 1886 in Kharkov, Ukraine of wealthy parents who employed German and French governesses for their children, Karinska had a privileged childhood. Intricate embroidery became young Karinska's passion, a passion that would be reflected in her future calling. Leaving Russia after the revolution, she established her own atelier in Paris and Monte Carlo, then London, and, finally, in 1949 she immigrated to New York City. On the occasion of being the first costume designer to win a Capezio Dance Award, her costumes were described as "visual beauty for the spectator and complete delight for the dancer." Her last work, at the age of ninety, was for Balanchine's *Vienna Waltzes*. She died at the age of ninety-six in 1982.

At seventy years old—when I first saw her—she was elegant, commanding, and, clearly, highly skilled. I watched in awe as she oversaw the last fittings. Pointing, pinching, and tucking, she gave instructions to the seamstress as we ballet girls stood in pink tights, damp and dirty from having come from rehearsal. I, and perhaps I was alone, felt more comfortable dancing in a costume whose bodice was more loose than tight. Intimidated by Madame Karinska, I said nothing. My solution was to expand my chest during the first measurements, hoping for a costume less tight. That I got! My costume swam around my bony frame and— still intimidated of course—I said nothing.

During my two years at the Met, Karinska costumes were made for four of the opera ballets and while in the Joffrey Ballet and American Ballet Theatre I had been fitted for eight others. By that time, I had ventured a meek and successfully respected request for a fit friendly bodice. I was amazed that in *La Traviata*, the lowly supers—for all practical purposes only part of the scenery—would be wearing costumes costing the astronomical sum of two hundred dollars. As I stepped into my ball gown with its wide, hooped skirt and its lace, pleats, flowers, and flounces, all meticulously stitched, I easily stepped into the world created by the powerful beauty of Verdi's music and Renata Tebaldi's voice.

Another new production during the 1955-56 season was Jacques Offenbach's *Les Contes D'Hoffmann* or *Tales of Hoffmann*. The third act of *Tales of Hoffmann* celebrated Hoffmann's third great love, a nineteenth century courtesan. Rise Stevens as Giulietta, along with the chorus and ballet, was dressed in folds of sumptuous velvet. The setting was appropriately sensuous. Deeply tufted sofas, thickly folded draperies, and scattered oversized pillows melted in rich dark colors. With an empty champagne glass in hand, I lounged with other velvet clad companions as the curtains opened and the intoxicating melody of the barcarolle, a Venetian boat song, flowed from the orchestra. The soprano's lilting aria joined to fill the air. Swelling up, the sound seemed to envelop me in waves of ever more velvet.

An opera, or rather three, that caused particular excitement was Wagner's *Ring Cycle*. German born Martha Moedl, a renowned Wagnerian soprano, was the star. "Rhinegold," the first opera in the cycle, opened onto a scene representing the bottom of the Rhine River and three swimming Rhinemaidens guarding a slab of enchanted gold. The actual Rhinemaidens were singing offstage. Three ballet dancers swam in their stead. We were hooked up to ropes, which were, presumably, invisible to the audience. Stationed in the wings, stagehands pulled us back and forth and up and down. Our waist length hair, entangled with streamers of seaweed-like material, trailed down our backs. Flowing, mottled-blue costumes hid the heavy leather harnesses that fit extremely uncomfortably between our legs and chafed up around our torsos. We were given the artistic freedom to improvise our own balletic, stylized swimming strokes. Because the motion through space felt like flying, we had to continually remind ourselves that our arms were not wings, but arms, albeit otherworldly arms, that needed to look as though they could have realistically, though theatrically, propel a Wagnerian Rhinemaiden through the depths of a murky river. (A twenty-first century production employs state-of-the-art trapeze wires, enabling Rhinemaiden singers to both swim and sing in relative comfort, a feat quite unlikely with the Met's 1950s technology. Mimed swimming in the Rhine was tour de force enough.)

Neither dancing in an opera ballet, singing in a little boy's chorus, nor being a super had the cachet of floating across the stage as a sylph or a willi, but they did give me opportunities to be familiar with two of the country's major opera houses. The old world elegance of both the New York Metropolitan Opera House and the Boston Opera House made each stage entrance reverential. Becoming familiar with the backstage areas in each of these houses made me feel as though I had found my privileged place in a procession of artists.

The dressing rooms of both the great opera houses were similarly located. The men dressed on one side of the stage and the women on the other. The dressing rooms for the stars were on the stage level and the soloists' dressing rooms were on the second and third levels. The stars and soloists were called "artists." Next, on the fourth level were the "chorus ladies." The "ballet girls" dressed on the same floor as the chorus at the Met and on one floor higher in Boston. Beyond the top floor, a spiral wrought iron staircase curled up to the rafters.

The 1956 Metropolitan Opera spring tour—the last before the Boston Opera House was torn down—gave me the opportunity to dance on the stage of my childhood dreams. My family was in the audience sharing in my good fortune. We opened with *Aida*. There was plenty of room (one hundred and thirty feet of vertical space) for lifting and lowering the massive sets, from throne to tomb. A friend and I stood in the wings, looking up. "I know a secret way to get to the other side of the stage," she whispered. Our dance had finished early in the opera. We had changed into leotards and toe shoes to practice those turns and steps which we hoped, one day, would take us from a pseudo Egyptian dance with the Met Opera Ballet to the world of willis and sylphs in a proper ballet company.

I followed my friend to the spiral iron staircase. Arias of the last scenes of the opera were soaring into the air. Holding onto the cold railing in the semi darkness, we circled up and around. Many narrow steel steps and six spirals later we reached the catwalk. We were seventy feet above the stage. "Come on," my friend urged again. Gingerly, we put one satin foot in front of another. Here, the railing was not only cold but it was very dusty. I focused on the steel grids under my feet. Spaced about two inches apart, the grids stretched fifty feet ahead of us, the width of the stage. Every few feet there was a reinforcing horizontal grid. An occasional vertical grid, freed from one or the other side of its horizontal mooring, dangled downward leaving a four-inch gap. Four inches is plenty enough room through which a dancer's squished pink satin foot can fall. The dust on the grids was thick and soft. Each of the seemingly endless steps we took precipitated a flurry of particles, which, when reaching stage level, caught light emanating from Aida's tomb. Looking through the grids, Aida and Rademes appeared to be about three feet tall. They sang and gestured and sang and posed as we continued inching along.

Finally, we took our last precarious steps arriving from stage right to stage left and to safety. The shining dust particles ceased to fall. Aida and Rademes sang their last measures of love. And, happily, they were not interrupted by the tragic end of two ballet girls.

Aside from following my foolhardy friend, I learned many valuable lessons from my older and more experienced colleagues. It was from them that I learned how to apply make-up, comb Vaseline into my hair leaving it both shiny and strand-free, and, most important, how to thoroughly secure ribbons on pointe shoes assuring that they would remain flap free. I learned to respect my costumes and the women whose job it was to clean and care for them. These same women dressed us. Forcing the back of a bodice together, they pulled one hook at a time, hook and eye, twelve or more times. We felt fingers march up our spines from the waist. I learned how to take good care of my costumes. Once dressed I neither ate, drank, nor sat. Costumes were never, ever, flung over a chair. Tutus were hung upside down, by the crotch so when turned upright the rows of ruffles would not sag. Costumes were expected to last for years. Dancers who had preceded me had worn many of

The Metropolitan Opera. The author, in La Perichole. *(From the collection of Marie Paquet-Nesson)*

mine. Block-printed with indelible ink, their names had been crossed out. Seeing my name freshly printed, dark and clear against the worn waistband, I wondered about those earlier dancers. Years later while watching *Turning Point*—the 1977 film starring Mikhail Baryshnikov, Shirley MacLaine, and Anne Bancroft—I realized that someone was probably wearing a costume that had once been mine during the *Swan Lake* segment. (Did the dancer in the film, whichever swan she may have been, wonder about me?)

I learned many lessons during my two years at the Metropolitan Opera Ballet Company. Some I learned from a difficult taskmaster, my own experience.

Chapter 6

THE MASKED BALL

Verdi's *Un Ballo in Maschera (The Masked Ball)* marked one of the first few times I had stepped onto the great Met stage. Eight ballet couples, most of the seventy-eight (or so it seemed) chorus of men and women, and the stars of the evening—Roberta Peters and Robert Merrill—had taken their places. Waiting for the curtain to open onto the masked ball scene, we were suspended mid-way in party appropriate movements. Heavy baroque wine glasses were held high, smiles glistened, and gestures froze in the air. Our eighteenth century style costumes were extravagant; our masquerade masks were nearly as ornate.

The curtain—every golden ton of it—opened slowly revealing the darkened stage. For several seconds both the performers and audience were still. Rows of ghostly faces stretched before me, an endless field gently sloping up and away from the orchestra. The conductor's baton was raised. Five tiers of seating were densely carved and faintly glittering. Horseshoe shaped, they framed the interior with a big open hug. The scene before me looked unreal, like a giant pop-up greeting card. We, on the stage, however, seemed very real even though we were motionless and wore masks and costumes.

The conductor lifted his baton higher and in one dazzling moment there was light, heat, music, and movement. The light was blinding. It came from foot lights, spots in every wing, and megawatts hidden from above. The heat from the light was immediate. The music was lush and enveloped us as we smiled and gestured, sat and stood, sang and danced. Roberta Peters and Robert Merrill were downstage, center. They would soon be singing an important duet. "I am going to catch you." "No, you are not." "Yes, I am." That was the gist of it. It sounded amazing in Italian.

My partner and I were directly behind the stars. Our dance was stately. Step together, we faced each other. Step back, side, front, our arms entwined from the elbow. And then, we held an elegant pose. For dramatic effect the stage had, once again, become a tableau. Not one hand or head moved. Even eyes, masked as they were, dared not wander. Nothing should divert the audience's attention from the stars. The duet began.

At the conclusion, Roberta Peters as Amelia, was to rush off stage and Robert Merrill, her King Gustav, was to be stopped from following and embracing her by me! Me! A brand new ballet girl! It was I who would break first from the tableau and run in a direct line downstage to keep our operatic lovers apart. Then, the rest of the company would move out of their poses to resume dancing and singing. Only poor King Gustav was to be left in place, watching as his beloved disappeared from view. I had anticipated this moment from our first *Ballo* dance rehearsal. There would be no full company stage rehearsal for this opera. Only new productions were allotted time and money for such a luxury. I knew the music would sound very different with a full orchestra than that of the piano arrangement we used in rehearsal. I was apprehensive. My partner, Adriano, assured me that he would help.

Adriano was twenty-six or twenty-seven years old and, obviously, a man of experience. As one of relatively few straight dancers, he never preened long before having a girlfriend or two. I was feeling womanly, having just been given a delicately robust part in the upcoming *Merry Widow*. When Adriano said he would cue me by a pinch on the tush, I smiled my consent. The day had come. The curtain had opened. The stars were singing. My moment was approaching.

Adriano found flesh through my voluminous skirt and petticoats, success I attributed to his Latin blood. I went charging down towards the singers with my eyes intent on the very small space between them. I wondered, briefly, why they were not parting and I wondered, even more briefly, why Roberta Peters turned to look at me. Her eyes had widened with surprise. But I was a woman on a mission; I absolutely must separate them. A determined jab with my elbow into the side of Miss Peters proved successful. Passing between her and Mr. Merrill, I continued down towards the footlights, made a wide and graceful arc away from the audience and faced back, upstage, where I had left my partner. To my horror, all the singers and dancers were still motionless. Roberta Peters and Robert Merrill were repeating, "I am going to catch you." "No, you are not."

I was the only moving creature on the grand old Metropolitan Opera stage. The stars were still singing and I was a full fifteen feet away from Adriano. Bent from the waist in a gentlemanly bow with one arm and leg outstretched towards me, he smiled apologetically. Frantic to get back to my place as quickly as possible, I took rapid little steps all the while hoping that I looked courtly. I slithered back into my pose. Some measures later, after the singers truly did finish, I started out again. It was a very embarrassing journey.

That night, I cried for hours, certain that I would be fired and that my promising career had come to an end. Although I was told that Roberta Peters was looking for "that ballet girl," no one said a word to me. My career was not over.

Chapter 7

TEETERING

It was New Year's Eve, December 31, 1955. A celebratory bottle of tequila was passed around the dressing room as we prepared to perform *Soiree*. The ballet's premiere had been only a week earlier. First-performance, anxious energy still beat in our hearts.

Soiree, the new ballet by our choreographer, Zachary Solov, was a departure from our usual dancing fare. First and foremost it was a bona fide ballet, not an opera ballet in support of the royalty, peasants, heroes, and scoundrels of the Metropolitan's grand operas. Having a ballet choreographed and performed in a double bill with a new production of Donizetti's comic opera, *Don Pasquale*, was seen as a commitment on the part of the Metropolitan Opera Executive Director, Rudolf Bing, to us, the ballet company!

Ballet stars had been hired to headline our roster: Mary Ellen Moylan and Oleg Briansky. The ballerina felt almost like a friend. Her picture, torn from a Ballet Russe de Monte Carlo program book, had been one of many that had hung salon style in my Boston bedroom. As a young teenager, I gazed into her beautiful face and imagined that I would one day, dance like her. Our first names, hers in English and mine in French translation, were the same, giving my wish extra weight. I was not fully aware that neither my legs nor my feet were, or would ever be, as long or shapely as hers.

However, it was 1955 and here we were, she and I together. We were dancing in the same company—albeit she was a guest ballerina and I was a lowly corps dancer—taking the same company classes, and performing the same ballet; she in white with a famous, handsome, male partner and me in the back line, one of many wearing orange. At that moment, just maybe, I thought, I would get close. Time and dreams were on my side. I was still a teenager.

Soiree was choreographed to reflect the same mid-nineteenth century time period as the setting of *Don Pasquale*. The ballet, done to the Benjamin Britten score *Soiree Musicales* (after Rossini), featured a romantic pas de deux danced by my namesake and Mr. Briansky, along with several peasant style divertissements. The "Tirolese," "Tarentella," and "Bolero" were each set for a small number of dancers. I, along with the remainder of the corps, joined them in "Moto Perpetuo," the finale. As "Moto Perpetuo" suggests, the last divertissement sped to the ballet's conclusion with quick footwork and quicker turns.

This, my first New Year's Eve away from my family and on my own in New York City, would become the most memorable. How could there be a more perfect way to bring in a new year than to be dancing in a pointe ballet on the stage of the Metropolitan Opera House?

I was already feeling a little giddy with excitement when the bottle of tequila made its way to my side of the dressing room. Determined not to appear as young and unsophisticated as I clearly was, I accepted it. "Is this Mexican wine?" I asked. "Sort of," the answer came in the direction of the "fast" girls—the sophisticates who all sat on the other side of the room; the ones who would hang up their tutus that evening and pour themselves into slippery cocktail dresses. These were the girls who attended fancy parties with management and top tier opera stars. When I first joined the company one of them had told me that I had been noticed and asked if I wanted to be included. Although I hated to be thought of as provincial, I was appalled by the suggestion. "No thank you," I had replied.

But a small paper cup full of wine on New Year's Eve? "Thanks," I called back as I lifted the clear and unpleasant smelling liquid. "Thanks," I said again, hoping that my voice had a hedonistic ring to it. Skirting the edge of naughtiness was fun.

At eighteen years old, I could legally drink and I had—two or three times. Each time it was for menstrual cramps, a remedy suggested by my friend, Maria. On each occasion it was before rehearsal and Maria would accompany me. Directly across from the stage entrance was an old German bar and restaurant, a haunt for opera buffs and performers alike. Covering the walls were generations of singers' autographed black and white publicity photos. Messages of thanks for good food were scrawled along the bottom of the photos. I liked being in the restaurant; I liked standing at the bar. It proved my adult status and the shot of brandy warmed my tummy while having only minor effects on my pliés.

The tequila wine, however, sent fire into my chest and air whirling around my head. This was a new and frightening experience. "Oh, my God," I exclaimed both in panic and sincere religious fervor.

My pointe shoes were tied and my costume had been hooked up. "Places" had been called. Those of us who had not already drifted down to the stage picked up the pace: a final pull on our tights and an additional ribbon check on our shoes. Two trips in the freight-size elevator later brought us all to the wings.

I prayed that it was not obvious, but I knew that I was incapacitated. I would not be able to execute any beats (those jumping steps which require the legs to beat together one, two, or more times before landing) or do any, except for the very simplest, turns. During the remaining minutes I had left in the wings, I set out on a plan to fake it. I would eliminate all the batterie (French for beats) and, instead, take a cautious jump up and an even more cautious landing. I would execute the traveling turns with less speed and change the double turns into singles. Ready or not, I took my place with the company. Being in the second and third rows was a fortuitous aid to the success of my plan.

The ballet was nearly over. Miss Moylan and Mr. Briansky were doing solo steps and lifts while the corps was grouped behind them. Some of us were posed on our knees and others of us, including me, were standing, legs and feet together, balancing on our toes. As I began to set my feet, legs, body, and arms for that last challenge, I glanced into the wings. Antony Tudor was watching! The famous choreographer! One of my (feared) teachers! His eyes were made of iron, all dark and hard. Had he seen that I was not dancing full out? Did he notice that I was moving about in what was supposed to be a still pose? Would he suspect my inexcusable inebriation? I willed my body not to respond to my swaying vision. I redoubled my efforts at slowing down the little toe steps that I used to maneuver my balance in order to stay up, however imperfectly, on pointe.

At long last, *Soiree* came to a close. I must have blended successfully enough with my colleagues; neither Mr. Tudor nor Zachary Solov and his ballet mistress said anything to me. I had survived another close call. This one—unlike the earlier upstaging incident—was entirely and undoubtedly my fault. (When the *Soiree* sets and dancers were cleared from the stage, the program continued with *Don Pasquale*. As fate would have it, the star was Roberta Peters, the surprised soprano from *The Masked Ball*. Even backstage, I avoided passing close to her.)

Four years later, in 1959, while with the Joffrey Ballet, I danced in another ballet to some of the same Benjamin Britten arrangements of Rossini music. Having been choreographed twenty years previously by Antony Tudor, it was similarly titled *Soiree Musicale*.

I finally realized that Mr. Tudor's particular interest in the New Year's Eve performance of *Soiree* was to critique Zachary Solov as a choreographer, not in judgement of the dancers—perhaps another aid in the concealment of my impairment. Although I never did resemble Mary Ellen Moylan, or achieve her technique and status, I could pretend that I was in her shadow; not on the Metropolitan stage in *Soiree* but on many, mostly small town stages, in *Soiree*

Musicale. I danced the ballet's romantic pas de deux, had a handsome partner, and I wore a white tutu.

Chapter 8

UNDERSTUDY

I was an understudy for twelve corps de ballet dancers in *Die Fledermaus*. If I was tempted to wish unwell the first cast of a coveted solo role, it was with enthusiasm that I wished good health and strong ankles to each of the twelve *Die Fledermaus* dancers.

Of the two dances I was assigned to learn, one was a can-can. Combinations of turns and kicks dazzled. Multi colored skirts and petticoats swirled and swished around the dancers' legs and over their heads. Legs clad in black silk stockings and arms clad in black lace gloves moved and waved and gestured as one. The can-can looked alive, like a strange giant centipede propelling along until the last high kicks and sudden splits to the floor. As we held the last pose, our skirts followed, billowing and fluttering to a leisurely finish. The energetic can-can was easy to learn. The patterns were straightforward and all the dancers were pretty much doing the same thing at the same time. "Going in" for any one of the dancers when the choreography consisted of four-of-this and eight-of-that was not a difficult assignment.

However, learning the second dance, the waltz, with its complex configurations seemed overwhelming. To keep out of the way during rehearsals, I stayed at the back of the studio to watch, learn, and practice steps, stage patterns, and timing. Following along, just as I had almost learned a segment, "Voila!" the music, choreography, and dancers had moved on. All twelve of the female dancers were dancing in a circle, then six moved here and six moved there. Three were lifted onto their partners' shoulders (called shoulder lifts) while three others were lifted in different poses and the remaining six dancers went into a different direction all together. The twelve male dancers then moved into a diagonal line from the backstage right corner to the downstage left corner. The female dancers peeled off to make another circle, now into two rows, now with partners separated, now leaping towards each other, and now away. Confused, I stopped. I began again but found myself in the way. I moved further back and to the other side of the room where I began watching the dancers on the opposite side. I needed to know both sides, I reminded myself. It was the same choreography but reversed. Why is it, I often wondered, that a series of steps done to the left side feels so foreign? It's as though a stranger's body is at work or, more precisely, not at work. My mind wandered. I stopped and stood by, watching numbly.

An understudy is expected to know a part well enough to fill in wherever and whenever needed, an important mark of a professional. My performing experience consisted of three weeks at Radio City and the Alicia Langford Ballet School concerts. In Boston there were no understudies; we were all in everything. At Radio City I was hired as the replacement.

Rarely does a corps de ballet understudy get a rehearsal. Even more frightening is being "thrown in" a ballet, an apt term for being put on stage at a moment's notice. I was profoundly grateful that this did not happen to me. When the ballet mistress said, "Marie, you do *Die Fledermaus* for Nancy at tomorrow's matinee," I had an overnight to prepare.

"Help!" I called to Maria Grandy, one of my new friends. "OK," she said. As a first cast *Die Fledermaus* dancer she had already performed the ballet several times. She agreed to come to my apartment that evening to teach me the part.

Before getting started, I prepared a thank-you dinner for her and Laurie, my roommate, who had generously agreed to relinquish some of her sleep that night. After yanking packages of hamburger patties and French fries from the fridge's tiny freezer (a freezer so frost-caked that it was fast becoming useless), I defrosted and cooked the food. Served with boiled broccoli, a glob of melted Cheese Whiz, and ketchup, we proclaimed it tasty.

We pushed aside the apartment's meager furnishings. Maria and I were both wearing slim-fitting mid calf-length pants called "pedal pushers" in Boston and "Capri pants" in New York. We did not need practice clothes. We would be marking, or indicating, the steps for memory and timing only.

Singing the music as she taught me the steps Maria quickly reviewed the can-can and then launched into the waltz. Minutes, quarter hours, and half hours passed as she patiently and doggedly kept to the task. I learned the steps, music, timing, and the general patterns. At eleven o'clock my friend—now my best friend—left.

I pulled the covers under my chin and stared up into the ten-foot ceiling. Flanked by wavelets of peeling paint was a dull brass chandelier. All the bulbs, save one, had burned out before I had moved in. A defective light switch kept the remaining bulb on day and night. The light was dim. It served as a twenty-four hour night-light. It didn't bother us.

As I tried to sleep, I saw myself dancing the waltz again and again. Each time I came to a section, direction, or step about which I was unsure, my body stiffened. Just as in reciting a poorly understood prayer or a poem in a foreign language, I did not trust myself to start from where I had left off. I needed to start over again from the beginning. Glitch, panic, start over, glitch, panic, start over and so it went until, eventually, I fell asleep.

The next day I went early to the theater. I passed the German restaurant. My stomach was too queasy to stop in for lunch.

The stage door of the old Metropolitan Opera House was unremarkable. Inside, three shallow steps led to a darkened corridor where a never smiling, large, older fellow sat at his desk. Light from a lamp with a shabby shade shone under his chin like an unflattering footlight for the face. He nodded either in greeting or permission for entrance. I never knew which.

I punched the time clock. Ballet companies don't have time clocks, however, the Met not only had a time clock, but posted time sheets were also pinned to a bulletin board, letting the singers and dancers know at what time they were required to be in the theater. It was not necessary to be in the theater for an eight o'clock curtain if the chorus or dancers were not in acts one, two, or three. Time sheets were useful guides.

The freight elevator took me to the ballet girls' dressing room. The elevator operator looked annoyed at having to get up out of his chair to shut and open and shut again the heavy door. He would look annoyed for the duration of his shift.

I was first in the dressing room. I put on my make-up robe, a duster bought from a Woolworth's five and dime store. It was cotton, shapeless, and knee length with buttons up the front. Housewives bought dusters to wear while doing housework. Mine was worn for magic, the act of transforming myself into a nearly very glamorous young woman. I sat at my dressing table, a three-foot section of a long built-in table that ran along each of three walls.

Each dancer had a mirror framed with light bulbs and a switch that was controlled individually. Our dressing tables reflected our personalities. The space to my right was clearly and neatly marked off with a sunny, pink cloth mat. It belonged to a dancer who generally wore her favorite color right down to her underwear. Her smile was sunny. On my left sat Maria. We were less rigid about our borders. We, along with most of the dancers, had good luck mementoes: hand-painted wooden or porcelain boxes in which to put stage rhinestone earrings, paper fans, ceramic puppies or kittens, and snapshots of families and boyfriends wedged into the mirror's edges. All the dressing room tables had identical, sturdy metal chairs. Leaning back, legs up on the table, coffee, and, for some, a cigarette in hand, we enjoyed moments of rest and camaraderie. These were my first experiences of deep contentment.

I turned on my dressing table's lights and took a critical look in the mirror. Scrubbed, my face became a canvas. One by one, I opened jars and pots and tubes of sticky color. Brushes of varying thickness poked out of a glass etched with a likeness of the Empire State Building. The brushes along with my fingers and make-up pencils were my tools. Although the relatively new pancake base make-up could be applied quickly with a dampened sponge and had gained popularity in our dressing room, Rosie, the veteran dancer who taught me the mysterious art of make-up, dismissed it. "A pancake base is flat," she said. "Grease paint is translucent and more beautiful under the glare of stage lights." I dutifully squeezed out one half inch of rosy beige from the tube and blended and rubbed it into every pore of my face and neck. Rosie also recommended heavily outlining lips, brows and lids. She showed me how and where to put dots of red and white to bring out the eyes and how to apply brown to emphasize cheekbones. The glamorous result was mask-like. "It will carry," she said, "to the back of the house." Another make-up trick was to leave little blotches of dabbed powder on the face, making us look a little like clowns. After doing a last warm-up barre hanging onto backstage ladders or practicing a difficult step one last time, the resulting sweat would have absorbed most of the powder. Before curtain we smoothed out the rest.

On this matinee day, with powder blotched in place, I put on practice clothes and walked up the stairs to the practice studio. No one was there. I did a barre. By the time I returned to the dressing room, the other dancers had arrived. The circular metal clothes rack in the center of the dressing room was laden with costumes for the matinee. Headpieces, hats, and flowers for the hair had been laid out on our dressing tables or hung from our mirrors. I would be wearing Nancy's costumes. Never slipping up, the wardrobe ladies had hung her costume by my, not her, table.

I put on Nancy's can-can costume, black silk stockings, and high-heeled shoes. Shaking out the layers of garishly colored ruffles, I left with the other dancers for the stage. The can-can was exhilarating. The choreography included a bit of flirting and that, too, was exhilarating. We held the final pose, the drop into a split, until the applause began to die down. We got up out of our poses in character and exited while throwing a flirtatious glance over our shoulders.

Back in the dressing room, we prepared for the waltz. This dance would be the first time I would be performing on pointe as a professional. (I discounted the experience at Radio City since the choreography was principally only running and posing.) Although most opera ballets were folk or court dances, there were others that were on pointe. Being on pointe meant that I had come of age, that I was a full-fledged, professional ballet dancer.

I took my Capezio, size 3D pink satin shoes off the shelf. I put my pointed foot down into the shoe. My toes crunched together and my fingers stiffened as I forced the shoe over my heel. Shoe on, I pressed my toes into the floor and tied the pink satin ribbons. The ribbons, one half inch wide, had been sewn inside the shoe keeping the outside smooth and sleek. Before being sewn, the inside ends had been folded over twice, strengthening them against any possibility of their ripping away. I tied the ribbons in a neat knot. After tucking the ends in the inside of my ankles, I wet them to prevent their slipping out of place. As an extra precaution, some dancers sewed them down.

I stepped into Nancy's waltz costume. We were the same size. The fitted bodice was laced with pearls and the over-skirt had ribbons sewn around the hem. As the back of the costume was being hooked up, I shook my head violently from side to side. Yes, I assured myself. No waltz turn or pirouette would dislodge my upswept hair or carefully pinned flowers.

Ten minutes had been called; five minutes had been called. Finally, a voice boomed over the loud speaker, "Places!"

A straggly parade of seemingly astral level creatures we were, as we stopped by the sinks just before answering that last call. In full make-up, hair slicked and adorned with flowers, we held up our layered crinoline skirts and effortlessly lifted our legs over the sink. Running the cold-water tap, we drenched the cloth heels of our shoes right through the pink tights. Not until we felt the cold on our skin were we convinced that the shoes and tights would stick together and not slip. On our way down to the stage we made little wet spots on the dressing room and corridor floors.

My partner met me in the wings. He smiled. "Don't worry," he said, so I didn't. (He was not Adriano.) And then we were on stage. Like a little wound-up dancing toy doll that knew what to do but not where to go, I relied on the guiding hands of my partner to keep my dancing within the parameters of the choreographic patterns. After being set down from a lift, or the end of a partnered turn, I felt a gentle nudge. Confidently, I sailed ahead and on and on until the dance ended. The ballet couples exited, waltzing into the wings. Off stage and breathless, I gave my partner a hug.

"Congratulations," Maria said as we ran up the stairs to the dressing room. "Thanks," I responded. We took off our costumes and hung them up. We took off our shoes, folded the heels inside and wrapped the flattened ribbons around each shoe once, twice, six times, and then tucked the ends neatly inside. One shoe fit snugly inside the other. This helped keep the shoes' shape as well as keep the ribbons from curling. We put our shoes back on the shelf to dry. If they were very damp, we might have taken them home and dried them in a 200-degree oven for a few minutes. Gobs of cold cream melted our make-up. Lots of tissues scraped it off.

We dressed and left the theater and went across the street for a late lunch. We talked about the performance, what steps we thought we could do better and which turns we thought we had done well. We then talked about our hometown teachers, the teachers we had at the Met Opera Ballet School, and others we had discovered elsewhere in the city. Dancers want to be challenged and encouraged. Above all else, they want to become better dancers.

Chapter 9

CLASS

Unlike a musician who picks up an instrument and learns how to play, a ballet dancer's instrument is her body, created by its training. Good or, at least, not bad training is essential. A badly-trained student will not be a dancer. And, cruelly, neither will a well-trained student not born with a "good" body. Since no body type is one hundred percent perfect, dancers every day and everywhere and at all levels send out wistful wishes for longer legs, higher arches, smaller rear ends, slimmer thighs, better turn-out, more flexibility, thinner, flatter, taller, shorter, younger or better in some way.

My friends and I were no different than thousands of other dancers in England, the Soviet Union, China, New Zealand, and Venezuela as we took our daily places along the barre. We stood at attention in first position and waited for the pianist's wrists to lift and the teacher to say "And!" We took a deep breath, expanding and lifting our chests. Our thigh and buttock muscles tightened and pulled up. Our necks turned and lengthened as we willed our spirits to assist us in a deeper and more turned out plié than that of the previous class. "And one," the teacher continued. The pianist's fingers fell on the first notes and our knees unlocked and slowly pressed out to form an ever more perfect ninety-degree angle from the hips. The class had begun. Dancers begin at the barre, doing a "barre" (French for bar).

Although the origins of ballet—as interludes of music and dance between courses at feasts—began in the courts of Italy in the Renaissance, it is generally accepted that it was at the court of Louis XIV where ballet began to grow and flourish. The Sun King loved to dance and was vain about his shapely calves and arched feet. Silk stockings and high heels, as well as turned out stances, showed off his royal limbs. Dance positions and steps were influenced by fencing positions, evolving court and even peasant dances. As the dancing became more complicated, professional dancers replaced courtiers. Just as ballet began with simple steps, pointe work also began simply, with a very brief touch of the toes to the floor. In 1832 Marie Taglioni, an Italian ballerina, danced the full two act *La Sylphide* on pointe. It caused a sensation. It is said that Taglioni's enamored fans cooked and, with a sauce, ate her shoes.

Barre exercises start with the right leg and then continue with the left. Alternating approximately twenty times, the barre is between thirty and forty-five minutes long. Feet point and stretch as they slide, strike, and brush against the floor. Legs bend, unfold, lift, and kick to the front, side, and back or in circular movements on the floor at forty-five degrees and in the air at ninety degrees. Backs are held straight or bent forward, to the side, or pressed back into elegant elongated arcs. Arms are held to the side motionless but never stiff, or move slowly to mirror smooth leg movements, and, with more difficulty, move slowly in contrast with staccato leg movements. The standing leg, or supporting leg, is challenged. It must be kept taut and stable to keep the dancer rooted and on balance. "You're off your supporting leg." "You're pulling away from your supporting leg." "You're sitting on your supporting leg." "Your supporting knee is bent." "Your supporting leg is turned in." These are the teachers' constant reminders.

Further challenging and strengthening the supporting leg is the "light only" pressure rule for the hand holding the barre. I had secret tiny calluses on the palms of my hands from holding onto the barre. Some teachers, making sure that we were not gripping the barre would come up from behind and suddenly pull our hands up off the barre. It was embarrassing to falter or, worse, to fall over. There was a collective sigh when the barre was finished. The large, industrial size studio windows were steamed over. The pianist stood.

We looked for the "thin" mirror and avoided the one we perceived as "fat." Even though we knew that mirrors not affixed completely flat against the wall resulted in a distorted image, looking at a heavier than normal reflection many of us dipped into depression while a thinner reflection would send our emotions flying. So, in front of the mirror we stood. Just maybe our thighs would look a bit slimmer than they did a few minutes earlier. We adjusted the leg line of our leotards. A little higher would lengthen the leg but too high would thicken it. We had favorite leotards. If they were all in the laundry and we were forced to retrieve that last one from the corner of the dresser drawer, we would have a bad class. For some dancers that would be the leotard on which the neckline was too high, the sleeves too short, or the cut around the leg too tight for any classroom readjustment. My last leotard choice was made of thick nylon and, after multiple washings, had been washed out into uneven black and nearly black splotches.

After the barre, the teacher asked the pianist to play an adagio. The teacher, if male and Russian, would probably have been smoking as he choreographed the exercise. Flushed and sweaty, we watched as we stretched. The teacher listened intently to the music as he made minimal gestures that we could read. The adagio, the longest combination of steps in the class, is thirty-two musical measures long and is repeated to the right and left sides. Of all the combinations in the class, the adagio requires the most balance and control.

We continued stretching. With the ease of a yawn, our bodies contorted into strange shapes. Legs lifted and slid along the barre and, holding the heels of our feet, legs were pulled into standing splits. We wondered how good we would look doing the adagio. How we felt about ourselves depended on it. This could change from combination to combination and even from step to step. The teacher finished and faced us. We tried to look unconcerned as he began placing us in groups for the center work. We faced him and the wall of mirrors.

Beside the incessant fat check, there are valuable reasons for looking at oneself in the mirror. A hip out of alignment will throw a turn totally off balance. An errant finger will betray tension and throw off the symmetry of an arm. Self-correction and experimentation are never ending.

The class is divided into two or three groups of two or three lines of dancers, depending on class size. The best and favorite dancers are placed in the first group. The worst spot is in the back line of the last group. The teacher calls the dancers in place, name by name or, disappointingly, with a "You" and a pointed finger. Teachers only remember the names of the dancers they like and consider talented. The center work, distinct from the barre, is done in groups and consists of complete dance phrases like little dances. The slow movements in the adagio are difficult; dancing them without any outward hint of strain makes them unquestionably more difficult. "Balance, balance, hold, hold," the teacher might coach over the music. "Lift the leg higher before the plié." A slow controlled turn, more difficult than fast ones, might follow. "Keep the back leg up." "Push from the back."

The remainder of the class moves quickly. There are fast turn combinations and jumping combinations and combinations that both jump and turn. The final combinations are the most exuberant and are often danced to a waltz. Large steps glide, jump, turn, and dart as they travel in long diagonal lines across the floor. "Push into, push off of, push away from the floor," the teacher calls. The impetus of a big waltz helps propel bodies into the air. Legs and arms fly to aerial poses. Spinning, one turn after another, the combination ends against the far wall into the wings of the studio practice stage. Then, the class is officially over.

The pianist, however, continues and plays something stately. The dancers, with sweat streaking down their faces, reverance (bow) to her as she continues playing. With a second reverance, they thank the teacher. The teacher says "Thank you," to the pianist and leaves the room. Standing aside, the dancers allow the teacher and pianist to leave the room first.

Many of our teachers went into the office to smoke and rest before beginning another class. The most esteemed teachers chose their pianists. Pianists who understood ballet vocabulary and the relative difficulty involved in its execution were prized. Teachers didn't want a symphony for a straightforward barre exercise. They didn't want unusual phrasing when the adagio was clearly designed in even segments. They didn't want a heavy 2/4 when a sprightly 6/8 would provide just the ballon (bounce) for small jumps and they didn't want a light waltz when something grander was needed to buoy up those last leaps.

A good pianist can make a boring class good and a good class great. A good pianist is able to dance in imagination as she watches and plays. A good pianist knows that a little faster and a little slower are in infinitesimal increments that have no musical counterparts. A good pianist knows what "a hair slower" means. Some pianists have music memorized, a few improvise, and some are weighted down with pounds of sheet music. Many have pasty complexions and look tired.

We took classes from some of the great teachers of the day. Margaret Craske and Antony Tudor with the Metropolitan Opera Ballet School were British and trained in England. Their classroom demeanor was calm. Miss Craske, although attired in the traditional below-the-knee black jersey teaching skirt and soft pink leather teaching sandals, looked like a sturdy English matron. I would not have been surprised if she had walked into the studio wearing a wool cardigan and oxford walking shoes. She was a serious woman. Her classes were difficult in subtle ways and I tried to please her. One day, in exasperation, she told me that she would never again explain some salient point and if I did not understand, it would be my loss. I didn't understand, she never explained it again and it probably was my loss.

If Miss Craske confused me, Mr. Tudor terrified me. A renowned and highly respected choreographer, his most prolific work was done in the 1940s. Credited to be the first to create psychologically based ballets, their simplicity and power were legendary. Of that I would, in ten years time, experience first-hand. Mr. Tudor was tall, thin, bald, and elegant in profile and movement. His classes were beastly difficult. They always included multiple slow turns with one leg held high and, seemingly, never enough impetus to complete them. I only knew one dancer who could actually do his classes and even she looked awkward. Mr. Tudor could be cruel. "Monster," he called out one day in class. "Yes, you," he pointed to the back of the room to an earnest girl who, in spite of not having talent, never missed a class. Her name was Star and I can still see her face, first startled and then crestfallen. I never forgave Tudor.

I began going to mid-town Manhattan to study with Russian and Russian trained teachers. Anatole Vilzak and Igor Schewezoff had emigrated from Russia. Valentina Pereyaslavic was from Lithuania. She had been Russian trained and spoke Russian and we thought of her as Russian. She and all other female Russian teachers were addressed as Madame, automatically bestowing upon them a little extra measure of respect. Behind her back, we called her "Perey," "Madame Perey." Her classes were extremely strenuous and she was strict. While most teachers would be happy to see you practicing in a back corner between groups, Madame would throw you out of class. A tiny, thick dynamo of a woman, she would point her finger and yell, "You!" She and all Russian teachers, no matter how long they lived in New York, spoke little English. What they did say was spoken in blunt, thick accents and contained few nouns and fewer verbs. The message, however, was clear. Continuing her tirade and, this time pointing to the door, she would continue, "Close door, other side!"

There are some behaviors that annoy all teachers. Dancers, if displeased with themselves, are tempted to sulk away at the combination's end. Sulking, stopping prematurely in the middle of a combination, and, worst of all, leaving class without permission will pretty much jeopardize acres of built-up good will.

Once a week I took class from Anatole Vilsak. He was a kind man and never threw anyone out of class. His class was the dessert I allowed myself for having toiled with more demanding teachers during the week. If some classes left me depressed and thinking I was less a dancer than I was, Mr. Vilsak's classes left me thinking that I was really rather wonderful after all. He was a short man with an easy smile. He wore long slim pants, flexible leather shoes, and long sleeved, rippling silk shirts. A small silk scarf was always tied around his neck. He and his class flowed with an easy theatricality.

Madame Perey and Mr. Vislak taught at American Ballet Theatre's school on West 57th Street. American Ballet Theatre and New York City Ballet were the reigning American ballet companies. Ballet Theatre was launched in 1940 and Lucia Chase was its long time director. Ballet Theatre, primarily a touring company, was in direct competition with Ballet Russe de Monte Carlo, also a touring company. I grew up watching both on their visits to Boston.

Ballet Russe de Monte Carlo was an offshoot of Diagilev's famous Ballets Russes, founded in Paris in 1909. The Diagilev company boasted legendary collaborations with Nijinsky, Danilova, Debussy, Stravinsky, Chagall, Picasso, and Matisse, among many others. By the late 1950s, the Ballet Russe de Monte Carlo, based in the United States, was a shadow of not only the earlier Paris company, but of itself. No new ballets had been commissioned, nor were there new productions of the old repetoire. The director, musical director, wardrobe mistress, and some of the stars were Russian. Many American dancers took Russian sounding names.

The dancers in American Ballet Theatre, however, either kept their names or, if they were changed, they were changed into something that was not necessarily Russian. American Ballet Theatre did American ballets from choreographers including Eugene Loring, Agnes de Mille, and Jerome Robbins, and they were the only major American company to perform Tudor ballets. The company also did the classics such as *Swan Lake, Sleeping Beauty,* and *Giselle.* By the late 1950s, if not earlier, the company was more highly regarded than Ballet Russe de Monte Carlo. Unfortunately, neither company had the foresight to acquire permanent performance space in New York City when it was financially feasible. Year after year they continued touring coast to coast and rented theaters for brief New York seasons.

Another of my Russian teachers was Igor Schwezoff who had come to New York before the Russian revolution. He taught at the Ballet Russe School on West 54th Street. He was toweringly tall and had a flair for the dramatic. He owned two Borzois (Russian wolfhounds), the preferred breed for the royal entourage in *Swan Lake's* first act. Mr. Schwezoff and his Borzois—looking alike with their high foreheads and long, lean legs—took majestic walks down Fifth Avenue. I loved Mr. Schwezoff's classes. He "taught" a class rather than "gave" a class (terms dancers use to distinguish between active analyzing and correcting and simply providing steps with little input). Mr. Schwezoff taught while holding a riding crop that he used to prod a slack muscle or tap down a lifted shoulder. I looked forward to his occasional choreographic flings. Finishing an adagio, unusually, with fast turns and a lunge to the knee and an arm draped over the face, I saw myself destined to star in contemporary ballets choreographed especially for my unique dramatic qualities.

During my first two years in New York, most of my classes were with Mr. Schwezoff and Edward Caton. Mr. Caton taught at both the Ballet Russe and Ballet Theatre schools. His early training had been in Saint Petersburg where he studied privately with some of the same teachers who taught at the excellent state run schools. Edward Caton was a large boned, overweight, rather tall man of around fifty years. He did not wear the soft pliable shoes other teachers wore, but instead chose worn, clumsy, leather street shoes. He wore oversized khaki pants and a dress shirt half unbuttoned. When he walked, every fold of his lumbering body settled and readjusted. The rumor was that he had bad hips although he seemed to walk easily enough. His was not, however, a dancer's walk. It was heavy but soundless and had the surprising grace of an elephant's. It was also rumored that he had a throat operation. All kinds of rumors circulated about our teachers and I believed all of them. This one may have been true. Mr. Caton's voice was a forced, energetic, stage whisper. "Ladies and gentlemen, I don't want to be rude but that was dreadful!" he was fond of saying. His face, also in folds, creased into a perpetual frown. "Ladies and gentlemen, that looked constipated," his raspy voice continued. He was all bark and I loved him.

All of our teachers had been dancers. Their differing backgrounds and personalities determined their individual strengths. American dancers were criticized for not having a uniform style or appearance. A stage full of American swans may have moved as one but they might not have looked as one, as did the English swans trained at the Saddler Wells (now, Royal Ballet) or the Russian swans from the Kirov and Bolshoi theaters. This failing could also be our strength as we easily adapted to being cowgirls and cowboys or sylphs and princes.

The exception to American lack of uniformity was Balanchine's New York City Ballet. Balanchine had put his own peculiarly American stamp onto his Russian background. His choreography with its speed and, sometimes, quirky style was creating a new breed of ballet dancer. She was the sleekest and the most fleet-footed, accommodating both his geometric shaped and lightening fast choreography. At the time I became a young professional, New York City Ballet was less than ten years old and was fast rising as both distinctive and unequalled. New York City Ballet dancers were different. Many of the rest of us thought of ourselves as either superior or inferior. Either way, we were not one of them.

My sights were set on American Ballet Theatre, as were those of my Met Opera friend, Maria Grandy. With this our goal, we worked at becoming better and stronger dancers. Maria was enthusiastic about a new teacher she had discovered. His name was Robert Joffrey. Did I want to try one of his classes with her? We set up a time to meet.

Chapter 10

EARLY JOFFREY

Maria's and my second year with the Metropolitan Opera had ended. Every week we went to the midtown social security office to sign for weekly unemployment checks. Since the last four digits of social security numbers determined the day and time of appointments, I saw the same people week after week. Theater people were easy to spot. Dancers, actors, and musicians, even if they had just awakened and were disheveled, were attractively disheveled. Animated or glum, their voices were affected, showy, and entertaining.

Friendships developed across the long lines. I cheered for someone who was on his way to an audition and commiserated with someone who wasn't. Dancers were usually on their way to class. They hauled large dance bags containing shoes, leotards, tights, a towel, make-up, and deodorant.

Upon reaching the head of the line, we handed in a form with a list of dance or dance related auditions copied from a recent issue of *Variety*. "Yes, we went to the auditions," we lied. "No, we didn't get jobs." Every week we checked off the box that stated that we were unqualified, not without some truth, to do anything other than dance. Having been forewarned by more seasoned colleagues, none of us accepted non-show business jobs. Waiting on tables or typing meant that a job would always be available, leaving us unable to collect unemployment insurance. Having time and energy for classes was all-important. Classes made us better dancers and kept us in shape until the next company contract four weeks or as many as eight weeks hence. I thought of unemployment checks as unintended government subsidy for the arts.

On one particularly hot morning in July, I was looking forward to my first class with Robert Joffrey. I met Maria outside the unemployment office and we took the IRT express train to West 14th Street. She had been going to the studio at Sixth Avenue and Tenth Street for a week. Taking the IRT and walking the four short blocks and the one long block to Robert Joffrey's studio was a trip I would make many, many times over the course of the following nine years.

The Boston Arts Festival. (Center) Nels Jorgensen and the author, in the Sarah Caldwell production of Offenbach's Voyage to the Moon, *1958. (photo credit: Will Rapport)*

The Joffrey studio included a small rehearsal room where we warmed up before class and practiced after class, a large main studio where we took classes, and, clinging to one wall, curtained dressing rooms. A door in one corner led to the apartment of Robert Joffrey and Gerald Arpino. Jerry, Bob's friend and co-dreamer, was a dancer, future choreographer, and eventual director of what would be called The Joffrey Ballet of Chicago.

At one minute before the start of class, the apartment door opened and Robert Joffrey walked into the studio and began class. He was a short man (five feet, five inches) and had a muscular body, long back, and powerful legs. His swarthy looks came from his Afghan father and Italian mother. Bob's father was born in 1886 in Hazara, Afghanistan where his grandfather was the ruling khan of the village. Upon his grandfather's death in 1916, his father immigrated to America and took the name Joseph. Bob's mother, Mary, was born in northern Italy and was an amateur concert violinist. They met in Seattle where Mary worked at the restaurant Joseph owned. Their son was born in 1928.

Robert Joffrey, or Bob, as we dancers in the early years called him, looked even younger than his twenty-eight years. He was always neat and trim wearing short-sleeved white cotton sport shirts and black trousers. Upon entering the studio, his energy and enthusiasm went into immediate high gear and there it stayed. After class, he could not resist giving just one more correction and we eager dancers knew it. Staying after the class was finished, we practiced our turns, hoping to catch his eye.

Turns are some of the most difficult feats and dancers practice them unceasingly. A common cry from someone who had previously perfected a turn, was "I've lost my pirouettes," and from the men, "I've lost my double tours" (double turns in the air). Turns on one leg or the other, turning inwards or outwards with a leg up at the knee or held high to the side or low to the back, multiple turns traveling or multiple turns trying not to travel, we practiced them all. When turns went well, a dancer's day was well on the way to being a good one. If, suddenly and seemingly inexplicably, a dancer's turns toppled off course, a probable miserable day was in the offing.

Bob, an insightful teacher, had a unique ability to go beyond the standard corrections to the physics of the movement. For instance, a common correction to a dancer falling to the right in a right-turning pirouette is, "Don't try to go around too soon. Go straight up first." Although this certainly is more helpful than being told that one is falling to the right—already abundantly obvious—it is not always enough. Clearly one cannot throw oneself around before rising up on the leg that will be doing the turning, but if one really goes straight up there is no momentum for any turn at all. The impetus for the turn must begin from the bottom of the plié (bent knees position), the feet must torque into the floor and the thighs must press backwards. The dancer must both begin the turn and resist the turn before springing (or rising) upwards. "Natural" turners do this automatically. The rest of us depend on enlightened teachers.

Attacking a technical feat with just the right combination of control and abandon requires confidence. I knew dancers who, even though they had the required expertise, hesitated, and others, whose weaknesses were obvious, surged ahead. An American Ballet Theatre dancer with the long legs, perfect body, enviable technique, and impressive interpretive qualities that I envied, never neared her potential. On the other hand, there were dancers with physical and technical limitations who achieved beyond what I would have believed possible. (I envied them as well.) Bob believed that lack of confidence could be remedied by the actual experience of performing and he put this to the test early on with the men in his company.

For the men in the early Joffrey Company, nothing was more intimidating then performing Balanchine's *Pas de Dix*. The Glazunov score included a tunefully bombastic men's variation. Ballet afficinados were familiar with the showy finale. The four male ensemble dancers did a traveling jump, running downstage towards the audience. Across the stage, in a straight line, they stood in fifth position with feet turned out, one foot placed directly in front of the other. Each of the men, one at a time, did a solo jump. The music almost sounded as though it was shouting "And go!"

The first dancer jumped straight up, did two turns in the air, and landed back into the starting position, nailing the ending without a wiggle. Even the least experienced ballet audience knew what to expect next. The second dancer began his jump; dancers three and four stood waiting. "Ta dum," continued the Glazenov score. Jump, turn, turn, land, and hold, dancer number two finished his jump but faltered in the landing. Wriggling himself back into an upright fifth position, he smiled gamely in mock triumph. "Ta dum," off went dancer number three, jumping up in such a precarious angle that he only completed one and a half turns. Scooting around the last half turn flat-footed, his eyes finally found front. Dancer number four dropped all pretense of bravura. As the least secure of the group, his expression turned grim. He jumped and landed woodenly, causing him to stagger backwards. All four of the dancers were back on balance after a bit of a scramble and, with elegance almost restored, completed the last steps to a merciful conclusion.

No matter how poorly the variation was executed, Bob was insistent that his strategy of throwing his fledgling male stars into the deep end of the pool was the path to proficiency. After a three-month tour of one-night stand performances of *Pas de Dix*, the men's variation really did begin to look quite good most of the time. One dancer confessed, however, that even though he was standing in fifth position and dressed in white tights and black velvet jacket, he never completely got over the sensation that he was standing in front of a firing line. I guess Bob was not always confident either. "No men's variation tonight," we would be told as the bus rolled into Chicago, San Francisco, or Los Angeles. Performing in Evanston, Daly City or Santa Monica, however, the variation would be back in the program.

Towards the end of the long summer of 1957 and just before signing a third contract with the Metropolitan Opera Ballet, Bob asked Maria and me to join his company. We jumped at the chance, viewing the upcoming tour as experience toward a final goal of being accepted into another, larger ballet company. Taking a substantial cut in salary (from the reasonable sixty-eight dollar take home pay with the Met to something quite a bit less) and no pay at all for six rehearsal weeks, seemed ample reward for the opportunity to work with Bob Joffrey and to take his classes at no charge.

We were thirteen dancers rehearsing for this third Joffrey tour. It included five of the original six Joffrey dancers from what would be known as the "station wagon days." The expanded company would travel in the comparable luxury of a bus. Bob did not hold an audition, but chose us from his classes. I was nineteen and two of the dancers were in their early thirties. The disparity in age, size, and body type was greater then New York City Ballet, less than the Met Opera Ballet, and about the same as that of American Ballet Theatre. Any lack of skill or experience was compensated by enthusiasm and dedication. We performed with a youthful verve that was infectious and seemingly spontaneous. We were meticulously rehearsed. We rehearsed ballets currently in the repertoire as well as newly commissioned works.

A new ballet takes a lot of rehearsal time. Choreographers who come to rehearsals with steps and patterns previously worked out on other dancers, from written notes, or fresh from their imaginations proceed more quickly than those who rely on company dancers for ideas and inspiration. Working for the latter can be either rewarding or tedious. Working with someone with limited talent can be excruciating.

A great ballet can be enjoyed even if it is not perfectly performed. Not so for a poorly constructed ballet. The thinner the choreographic effort, the more is required of dancers to pull it off. Whether working through awkward transitions or forcing steps to cover unreasonably long or unreasonably short distances, rehearsals can eat up a lot of time. Dancers' patience may give way to sullen compliance.

On one tour we had such a ballet. It usurped many extra rehearsal hours that could have been used towards the rest of the program. The choreographer, an inexperienced young man, made vain attempts to inject creativity into standard steps and lifts. Instructing our partners to make the shoulder lifts more interesting by putting us onto their left instead of their right shoulders sent us all into a wave of eye-rolling. "Everyone does it on the right," he explained. Another eye-roll. (A shoulder lift looks like a shoulder lift no matter on which shoulder the ballerina is sitting, except that the chance of her being more awkwardly placed is greater if the partner is lifting in an unfamiliar way.) Watching the ballet's progress, Bob gave a diplomatic suggestion or two. Bob's dark eyes darted back and forth and his fingers drummed against his thigh, a clear sign of agitation. He was too polite to be rude and he expected as much from us.

Etiquette aside, this ballet was needed for our upcoming tour. Although we took an extra ballet or two as an occasional substitute, basically, we traveled with one program of four short ballets. Our newly commissioned work was to be one of them. The ballet's world premier, as it was noted in the program rather grandiosely (or so I thought), was premature. The ballet needed more work and more work it got. We rehearsed it night after night during our very difficult one-night-stand tour.

It followed our daily warm-up class and preceded the usual run-through of the evening program, last minute gulps of coffee, and a second short, pre-curtain barre. We felt imprisoned as we attempted to rehearse away awkwardness. One evening after having finished yet another rehearsal, one of the original "Joffrey Jets" (a nickname given to the station wagon pioneers) stormed off the stage. Although most of the rest of the company had been grumbling for weeks, she had been quiet and was, I thought, the perfect trouper. Much to my delight, she slammed the dressing room behind her, exclaiming, "Eighty hours we've spent on this fucking ballet!" Hearing her—of all people—use such language shocked me, but I never doubted the accuracy of her eighty-hour count.

Rehearsing with Bob was a very different experience. Repeating an aerobic passage until it had the quality he was seeking was exhausting but exhilarating. Even with a small group it takes many repetitions to dance in unison. Dancers doing identical steps can look different from one another. Not only the height of a dancer, but the ratio of limbs to torso, as well as the relative height in jumps and leg extensions can affect the timing and look of the choreography. Additionally, some dancers move more easily in lyrical passages and others in quicker movements. Bob wanted us to dance as one. We rehearsed full-out. When he said we could mark a section he only meant that we didn't have to smile through and project beyond the mirror, the ever present "pretend audience." Chests heaving and sweat dripping, we kept dancing for him as well as ourselves. Even rehearsing a lyrical and less strenuous ballet was exhausting in its own way. Rehearsing his own choreography, Bob worked and reworked every detail. "Try it with your hand here." "Try it with your hand there." "Try it again here." Bob was like a visual artist. Following his own vision, he sculpted his ballets on us. It was a privilege to work with him in this way.

Many rehearsals include partnering work. All female dancers value good partners and tall female dancers are doubly appreciative if their partners are also tall. Since jumps and turns—the stock in trade for male ballet dancers—are more suited to a short body than a tall one, many male dancers are not tall enough for the taller female dancers. Additionally, when a female dancer is on pointe, inches are added to her height, resulting in some comical match-ups. A male dancer struggling to lift and then hold his partner in the air or reaching up to grasp her hand for a balance, all the while keeping a smile planted on his face, is a predicament to be avoided if at all possible. This, however, is not always possible. If one is in the corps de ballet and dancers are in short supply, then one simply dances with whomever one is assigned. On the other hand, if a ballerina (a principal dancer, not a soloist or corps de ballet dancer) needs a tall and reliable partner, she could influence a dancer's promotion to premier danseur (the male equivalent of ballerina) even if he were not quite up to the usually required technical level.

Some men have an instinctual sense as to where their partners' balance is or will be. Imagine the difficulty of holding a ninety or one-hundred and twenty pound person in the air and then setting her gently down so that she is poised and balanced on one toe (or more accurately, on five of them crunched together). Now realize that, as you are setting her down, she is sliding close to your body so that you cannot see what you are doing. Having set her down, there are further intricate balances—the press of a hand (one into the other), the shift of a hand on a shoulder, and the manipulation of hands around her waist all have to be worked out.

A good partner can not only sense his partner's balance and enhance her turns, but can lift her with ease. He, in turn, is happy if his partner does not totally depend on him to keep her on balance, is capable of turning well on her own, and can jump with strength. More than once I've seen an inexperienced female dancer collapse in mid-air and, falling forward, cause her partner's wrists to twist. Losing his grip, the dancer tumbled to the floor and then blamed her partner for the fall.

The Boston Arts Festival. (Left to right) Francoise Martinet, Nels Jorgensen, and the author in Robert Joffrey's Pas des Deesses, *1958. (photo credit: Will Rapport)*

The most challenging lift I did was one that was preceded by a long diagonal run across the stage to my waiting partner. I stopped short of running into him by a sudden half-turn. My back to him, I bent my knees slightly and, keeping them bent, did a small hiccup of a jump. My partner, in a deep knee bend and holding his elbows close to his side for leverage, made a seat with his hands. He then pressed me above his head. Immediately, I pulled my knees up so as to be in a sitting position. Our timing had to be perfect. It helped that my partner was strong. He was that and he was tall. Sitting there, seven and a half feet in space, there was nothing in front of me except the red glow of an exit sign at the far end of the auditorium. It was frightening.

The only time I fell from a lift (or dropped, depending on one's point of view!) was the result of height differences between my partner and me. Often unavoidable, especially in a small company, dancers learn to compensate. The lift began with a jump into my partner's outstretched arms. I lay flat as my partner flipped me, pancake-like, up and over his shoulder. Instantaneously, he grabbed my ankles, and hung me over his back. I arched my head and arms far behind me and looked up and out towards the audience. Because I was too tall for my partner, I tended to stall against his neck. I solved the problem by grabbing his shoulder mid-flip and pulling my body up and over. The sequence of my jump, his catch, my clutch and pull, and his grasping my ankles worked every time, except once.

In one performance, the timing of my pull and his ankle grab was way off and I plunged down his back. I did not have time to put my hands in front of me, but held my wing-like position as I slammed into the floor, chest first. Gasping for breath, I left the stage. Weeks later, when a sharp pain in my ribs persisted, I finally went to a doctor. By that time the hairline fracture was almost healed. Not only did I not miss a performance, but also directly after the accident, I returned to the stage to finish the ballet.

At the end of a long New York rehearsal day, we closed ourselves into the curtained dressing rooms and carefully put our pointe shoes and ballet slippers into our ballet bags. (I had replaced my gray plastic hat shaped bag—popular in high school—with a sophisticated Italian leather import. Bought in a shop on Madison Avenue, it cost a week's Met Opera salary.) Sitting on the narrow bench, I peeled off my damp and sticky Danskin tights. The dirt and rosin from the floor had turned them black and yellow. The porous old wood floors we danced on held years of grime. They were washed weekly. Not only did the dirt continue to surface but also the floors, after they were washed, were a bit slick for a day or two.

Slipping is a dancer's fear. During class and rehearsal, we made trips to the rosin box, a roughly hewn wood box containing about a quarter inch of rosin. Every studio had a rosin box somewhere in a corner. Rosin, bought in large yellowish chunks, was hammered into smaller pieces. On the way to the barre or before rehearsal dancers ground them into powder. (Brittle and semi-transparent, the rosin dancers use is what remains after pine resin is heated and the liquid vaporizes.) Shoes that were old and caked with rosin felt safe. But if pointe shoes were new, we rubbed the soles of our shoes and ground the tips of our hard tipped pointe shoes into the rosin box multiple times. We hated the floor after it had been washed. But the weekly wash was routine and unquestioned.

It is not possible to dance without good traction. As in walking, in order to travel forward the back foot pushes into and away from the floor. There is a moment of being off balance until the weight has transferred, which is why walking on ice is so difficult. Pushing off the floor for a jump or onto the toes of one foot requires even greater traction. Occasionally in a small town, in an effort to please us, the stage floor would be washed and, to our horror, waxed. Our stage manager, if he had the time, would then slosh it with Coca Cola. That worked perfectly. The Coke ate right through the wax, and, incidentally, through the varnish finish—not something that our hosts appreciated.

The most dreaded surface, however, was an old wood floor with an oily base. Coca Cola did not work. Rosin helped, but made sticky patches. The men in their soft ballet shoes struggled with turning and, worse, the extreme friction made ear-piercing screeches. The women, however, would still be at risk. The edge of the hard blocked toe of the pointe shoe cut right through the rosined layers, leaving a skid mark on the stage and the dancer in a sudden hard fall.

Today, there are over a dozen companies that sell flooring appropriate both for touring and studio use. They range from rolls of thick, synthetic material to a floating system of "sprung" wood panels. Sprung floors have a base of basket-like woven wood slats over which the floor is laid. Not only are the floors not slick, but also they have a slight spring that protects against shin splints.

However, ballet pioneers danced on whatever floor had been laid. During one performance I fell three times, the most dramatic during a ballet in which three couples held hands and ran in a circle. It was a fast run. The circle needed to open out into two lines for the leading male dancer to appear from the wings carrying the female lead high above his head. Leaving a clear path was important.

I slid and fell, threatening the choreography. The other dancers were so intent on getting to their places that they didn't slow down enough for me to get back on my feet. Instead, they dragged me on my belly around with them. Not until the two lines were in place, was I finally able to stand. The ballet, a solemn one, continued. One of the couples walked off stage prematurely. There they were, my friends, in the wings, doubled over in uncontrolled laughter. Annoyed, I shot them a deadly glance. It did no good. They laughed harder.

We were in South Hadley, Massachusetts, one of the many stops on a three-month bus tour. After this one however, there was a surprise. We were told that we had been booked for the 1958 Summer Boston Arts Festival. It was another homecoming for me! Performing in an open-air theater did not have the romance of the old Boston Opera House, but I would be performing featured parts in a ballet company. The two ballets on the program were *Pas des Dessees*—one of Joffrey's signature pieces—and *Le Bal*—a sprightly Spanish inspired ballet, also a Joffrey work. The program included the "Nutcracker Pas de Deux" and the "Black Swan Pas de Deux," both performed by Andre Eglevsky and Mia Slavenska, two international ballet stars. The Festival had first hired them, as the draw, but we, the young Robert Joffrey Ballet, held our own, garnering equal numbers of good reviews.

Andre Eglevsky was a large boned man, not the physique one might expect of a ballet dancer. But he was an excellent dancer and partner for Mia Slavenska, a glamorous, if outspoken, ballerina. In her eighties, she was still glamorous and outspoken. (She is featured in the 2004 documentary, *Les Ballet Russes*.) The stars dressed, warmed-up, and rehearsed separately from us. They ignored us and we kept a respectful distance.

Fascinated, I watched Miss Slavenska rehearse. She was known for her formidable balances. Whereas most balancing ballerinas touch down sur le pointes (on the toes) for a couple of sublime seconds, Miss Slavenska could maneuver her foot and ankle like a ball bearing for many seconds, if not sublimely, then mightily.

A week later the company performed again at the Arts Festival for the first performance of Sarah Caldwell's newly formed Boston Opera Group. The opera was *Voyage to the Moon* by Jules Offenbach. This would be the first American performance and would be the precursor to Sarah Caldwell's presenting many little known or little performed works.

Bob Joffrey's choreography was light-hearted, as was the opera. Along with dancing, several of us had small acting roles. Signifying lack of gravity, I suppose, we traveled on and off stage by jumping up and down, causing the ping-pong-like balls atop the antennae on my head to bounce with me. More odd than sci-fi, the costumes were fantastical enough to inspire my few speaking lines. "Oh no, I'm scared," my Moon Princess character cried out, hands clasped on her chest, above a set of silvery orbs. Wearing a hat resembling an inverted RCA Victrola speaker, her partner, the Moon Psychiatrist, listened intently.

This was the first of a number of opera ballets in which the Joffrey Ballet would ultimately appear. Although I considered opera dancing second class, I was proud to dance with Bob's company. We were not opera company dancers on the payroll of an established opera company, but an independent, full-fledged though small, ballet company hired for specific operas. Thus, in my mind full of exalted dreams, we were guest artists.

Chapter 11

MORE OPERA AND BRIGADOON

Eager to keep his dancers together and dancing during long layoffs between bus tours, Bob choreographed for the New York City Opera Company. Among the operas I revisited were *Carmen, La Traviata,* and *Die Fledermaus.* (The Joffrey also performed during the fall of 1960 and in 1968 and 1969, at which times I was not with the company.)

No longer singing in the little boys' chorus, I danced in *Carmen* with two large red roses holding up my hair, ostentatious red and black ruffles whirling around my legs, and a lace shawl seductively wrapped around my shoulders. Instead of being a supernumerary guest in the party scene in *La Traviata,* I danced as an entertainer at the party. I was not a frightened understudy in *Die Fledermaus,* but a well-rehearsed and confident member of the ensemble.

Julius Rudel was the Austrian born and American trained musical director of the New York City Opera (a position he would hold from 1957 until 1979). Although he presented well-known operas, Mr. Rudel's particular interest was in non-traditional, contemporary operas, some of which were American. Among those were *Wuthering Heights* and *Susannah* by Carlisle Floyd (Phyllis Curtin, the first Susannah, joined us in a square dance, dosey-doeing quite smoothly); *Regina* (text from Lillian Hellman's *The Little Foxes*) by Marc Blitzstein; *Wings of the Dove* (based on the Henry James novel of the same name); and *Ballad of Baby Doe* by Douglas Moore, which had an American folk music sensibility. Having become accustomed to the well-established operatic repertoires of the Met, it had not before occurred to me that opera could and did adapt to twentieth century tastes. After all, I reminded myself, American Ballet Theatre's cowgirls and cowboys from *Rodeo* by Agnes DeMille and *Billy The Kid* by Eugene Loring easily co-existed among the more fey creatures that wore swan (most likely duck) feathers or see-through sylph wings.

Bob had the choreographic ability to adapt quickly to many styles. He could adjust to constraints of space and configuration of the stage. These skills plus the cohesiveness and energy of his small band of dancers contributed to happy opera collaborations. Although Bob labored over choreography for his own company, by both examining the larger stage patterns of intermingling, intersecting dancers, and scrutinizing the tiniest details of the actual steps, he tossed off opera ballets with ease. On a few occasions, this facility led to last minute choreography.

On one occasion, Bob's procrastination resulted in our rushing from the Greenwich Village studios to the City Center Theater on West 55th Street. We arrived for the first full stage rehearsal of *Merry Widow* on time, but not fully prepared. While Bob had only taught us the opening movements of the ballet just before it was time to wrap ourselves into our coats and hail cabs, he did not seem worried, but I was. Would Mr. Rudel, a maestro after all, be angry with us? "Do what you know," Bob instructed us, "and then just stand there and say nothing. I'll take care of the rest."

Mr. Rudel began conducting and we began dancing. The music of *Merry Widow*, a Franz Lehar operetta, was set at the turn of twentieth century Paris. It had a distinct Viennese flavor and we threw ourselves with gusto into the first strains of one of the well-known melodies. After what seemed like a very short time indeed, we stopped dancing and stood quietly, just as we were instructed. No fidgeting. No little nervous ballet stretch or bend. As usual, we were neat and trim, looking above

The New York City Opera. (Left to right) The author, Gage Bush, Francoise Martinet, and Dianne Consoer, in La Traviata, *1958. (From the collection of Marie Paquet-Nesson)*

reproach. Mr. Rudel put his baton down. The musicians stopped playing. Mr. Rudel looked puzzled. Bob leapt onto the stage and began talking through the rest of the choreography. It had not been fully taught to us, he explained. He gesticulated and pointed and waved his arms, all the while calling out ballet terms, in French of course, which added to Bob's authority. Mr. Rudel looked appeased.

By opening night, *Merry Widow* went well and Mr. Rudel was happy. Years later, it occurred to me that the reason we had not been taught the entire ballet had less to do with our not learning it and more to do with Bob's not having yet choreographed it. The theatricality of his presentation during that stage rehearsal was most probably an impressive bluff.

Further collaborations with the New York City Opera included performances at the Chautauqua Institute in upstate New York during the summers of 1959 and 1960. (Having taken a leave of absence in 1960, I participated in the first summer only.) The Chautauqua Institute is a National Historic Landmark. It was founded in 1874 by the Chautauqua Lake Sunday School Assembly as a center for summer learning. It included academics, music, art, and physical education. Today it is known not only for high quality classes in art, music, dance, theater, and writing skills, but also for professional level performances in symphony, chamber music, dance, and theater.

The Joffrey Ballet not only danced in Chautauqua with the New York City Opera, but also in our own separate programs. We performed our regular repertoire as well as two recently acquired ballets: the "Peasant Pas de Deux" from the first act in *Giselle*, choreography by Nicholas Sergeyev (after Marius Petipa) with music of Friedrich Burgmuller and *Soiree Musicale*, choreography by Antony Tudor with music by Benjamin Britten (after Gioacchino Rossini). Peggy van Praagh, who was artistic director of the Borovsky Ballet and instrumental in establishing the Australian National Ballet, set the ballets for us. In 1938, as a member of Antony Tudor's London Ballet company, she had danced in the original *Soiree Musicales*. We respected her background, knowledge, and even temper. (As Artistic Director of the Australia Ballet from 1963 until 1974, she would be honored with the title, Dame.)

Being cast in the "Peasant Pas de Deux" from the first act in *Giselle* made me feel as though I were inching into one of the most famous full-length ballets in the classical repertoire. There are many solo roles performed by second tier dancers in full-length productions and "Peasant Pas" is one of them. Generally, the complete *Giselle*, along with *Swan Lake* and *Sleeping Beauty* are only performed by major classical ballet companies with large casts of excellent dancers, extravagant sets, and costumes, and leading ballerinas of unquestioned status. Many little girls dream of

Paul Sutherland with the author, in "Peasant pas de Deux" from Giselle. *(photo credit: Will Rapport)*

being one of those ballerinas. Although even being on the same stage with one such being fulfills a portion of that dream, as I would ultimately discover. The pas de deux I danced was coquettish and was filled with buoyant jumps. The choreography was uncomplicated and included no difficult steps to dread. My partner and I breezed in and breezed out, enjoying every minute.

The second ballet, *Soirees Musicale*, an early Antony Tudor work that we irreverently referred to as his "teen-age period," was very different from the psychologically fraught ballets of his subsequent choreography. The series of dances: "March," "Canzonetta," "Tirolese," "Bolero," and "Tarantella" began with the entire cast of nine dancing the "March" before sitting in dainty, little chairs along the back curtain. In groupings of two and three, the dancers stood up to perform the charming dances that concluded with the full cast joining the "Tarantella" finale. Antony Tudor, himself, took over the last rehearsal. We were nervous. I imagined that Bob was too. Everyone knew that if Tudor was not happy with the way we danced, he would not give the company permission to perform the ballet. And, of course, his reputation for severity and sarcasm was in itself cause for apprehension. To my relief, he was both pleasant and helpful. And he must have had no objections because we performed *Soiree* many, many times over the next several years.

"Canzonetta" is light and song-like and it was to this that Tudor choreographed a lyrical, romantic pas de deux. As delighted I was to have been cast in it, my most vivid memory will always be my unforgivable mishap. It occurred on one of our bus tours without Bob. Bea Tompkins, our ballet mistress, was charged with correcting and critiquing us in classes, rehearsals, and performances. As Bob's representative, we knew that if we let her down, we let Bob down. We also knew that she reported back to Bob nightly.

My partner was costumed in classical white tights and velvet jacket. My tutu was three quarter length, white, and like most tutus, delicately decorated. The bodice was black velvet and had a set of short, fluffy, white sleeves. Full-bloomed white roses circled my head. We looked our parts perfectly. He was the attentive gentleman lovingly partnering me and I was the maiden who responded with a balance of chaste aloofness and warmth of feeling, not unlike a Jane Austen heroine. The pas de deux ended with my partner center stage on one knee with arms outstretched as though waiting, perhaps, for an embrace. As a gentle and elusive creature, I approached him from behind, taking tiny steps (sur les pointes). Preparing for the final pose, I took one last elongated step reaching out and up onto the tip of my left foot. Balancing on my toes with my right leg bent and lifted behind me (attitude derriere), my outstretched arms mirrored his perhaps as a promise of a future embrace. My eyes were cast sweetly downward.

The key to being able to balance without falling over throughout the last echoing sounds of the "Canzonetta" was correctly judging the distance to the back of my partner's shoulder against which I needed to lean. My partner assisted me by adjusting his kneeling stance either a few inches forward or back. If, however, I badly misjudged and found myself pressed much too close to him, there was little room for him to adjust. There was a limit as to how far forward he could bend! He could not, after all, end up with his chest resting on his knees. At a performance in a town somewhere either en route to the Pacific Coast or returning from it, I finished so close to my partner that I not only nearly folded over his shoulder, but I clunked down off my pointes.

At intermission Bea stormed backstage furious with me. It was not the clunk but what accompanied it that angered her. "I was in the back of the auditorium," she said, "Everyone heard you." "They did?" I asked mortified. Through my delicately parted lips, I had hissed, "Shit," totally destroying the mood of the ballet and probably shocking our small town, middle American audience.

Along with the New York City Opera and Joffrey performances, the 1959 Chautauqua summer featured the Lerner and Loewe Broadway show *Brigadoon*. Although I always preferred dancing in our company performances, I was excited to have been cast as Jean MacLaren, the young bride-to-be, in *Brigadoon*. It was another moonlight and roses role, this one requiring both acting and dancing. To the lilting "Come to Me, Bend to Me," Bob choreographed a dance for Jean and her friends that was tender and dream-like. It set the tone for the contrasting emotions in the subplot. (The main plot involves a twentieth century tourist who happens upon eighteenth century Brigadoon, falls in love, and chooses to stay.)

Brigadoon is a story of a hidden Scottish Highlands town that remains unchanged and unspoiled by existing in suspended time. Each morning dawns not only on a new day, but also on a new century. The spell remains as long as no one leaves the town. Harry Ritchie—played with ardor and drama by Jerry Arpino—is a troubled young man who becomes increasingly despondent over Jean's betrothal to another. He makes clumsy and tempestuous advances and Jean is frightened. Jean's scream, alarming the townspeople around her, further humiliates Harry. Distraught, he declares his hatred for Brigadoon and threatens to leave and end the town's idyllic existence.

This dramatic turning point called for a loud scream springing from Jean's panic and terror, not a self conscious squeak from a suddenly, stage frightened ballet dancer. Being asked to scream at the dress rehearsal had taken me by surprise. After my first weak attempt, Mr. Rudel stopped the rehearsal and gave me one additional try. When my second scream was equally ineffective, he again stopped the rehearsal. "You do it," he said to a chorus singer who was close by my side. And she did. From that time on, the scream had my opened mouth and her sound.

The author and Paul Sutherland (who was intent on keeping her from falling off her pointes), in Antony Tudor's Soiree Musicale *(photo credit: Will Rapport)*

The local Chautauqua paper said that I was "a shyly ardent bride-to-me and created considerable tension in the climax of the wedding scene. Most touching, was her 'Come to Me, Bend to Me' dance." I felt as though I did not fully deserve the good review.

However, we soon stepped off the operatic stage and returned to New York City.

Chapter 12

ON THE BUS

We were thirteen dancers strong on the first Joffrey bus tour. Every other seat had been removed, leaving space for a stool on which we could stretch our legs. How pampered this extra room made us feel! On subsequent tours the company grew larger and the buses grew correspondingly cramped. Comfortable bus travel became company lore.

During six seasons of bus tours, we would perform in over four hundred cities and towns, sixty-nine of them during this first one. On the morning of January 3, 1958, a silver bus with Robert Joffrey Theatre Ballet lettered along the side pulled up outside the studio door. Bob, who traveled with us on selected weeks, boarded with us.

Bob Joffrey was born in Seattle on Christmas Eve, 1928. From Mary Ann Wells, a local teacher, he not only received good ballet training but also an interest in dance in all of its forms and the history that went with it. He danced professionally for only six months, replacing an injured dancer with Roland Petit's Ballets de Paris Company while the company was on tour in Seattle. I would guess that the company—whose ballets were cinematic to the point of melodrama—was not what he had in mind for himself. He also had to know that his short stature would prevent his ever becoming a leading classical dancer. His passion for ballet drove him to start his own company. As both a knowledgeable dance historian who revered the past and a visionary who believed in his own future, Bob's optimism matched his energy. So why would many others and I not hook our stars to his?

I often looked forward to regularly scheduled meetings in Bob Joffrey's office. A small bust of Napoleon sat unabashedly on a corner of his large desk. Bob sat at his desk while we dancers shared the few chairs and spilled over onto the floor. There were nineteenth century ballet prints on the wall and a large photograph of the company's six original dancers. Over the years, more recent photos and tour posters were added. I recognized many of the pictures in an *Architectural Digest*

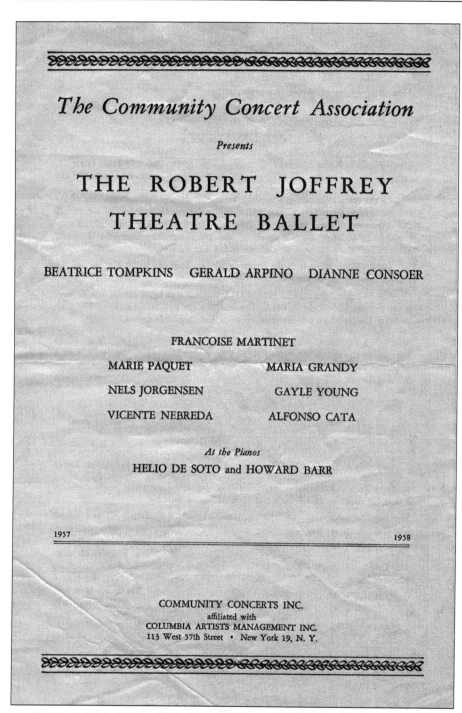

The Joffrey Ballet's third U.S. tour, (the first bus tour). Jonathon Watts, Brunilda Ruiz, and John Wilson joined later, mid-tour.

photo spread of Bob and Jerry's apartment more than two decades later. Did he talk about the early days of the company, I wondered, when guests came to visit? Did my name come up? Did he point out my picture? Did Bob say I had been a good dancer?

The gathering in Bob's office felt intimate. His telling us about upcoming work, tours, repertoire, and choreographers with whom we would be working seemed almost like secrets revealed. He predicted the growing interest in dance and its resulting "ballet boom" that took place in the 1960s. He believed that the United States, like European countries, would have a national company. It looked as though his prediction was correct when, a few years later in the early 1960s, a center for the performing arts in Washington, D.C. was in the planning stage. It was to be called the National Cultural Center. Before its completion, it had been renamed The Kennedy Center. A national ballet company never materialized, but back then I believed that it would. What a heady experience it was to envision Bob's company in that position.

When Bob traveled with us, he sat in the front seat. He worked through stacks of paper and correspondence. He never slept. Jerry Arpino sat in the seat behind, his head swathed in a black scarf. The scarf and his black hair contrasted sharply against a white pillow. The overhead luggage racks were head to toe with stretched-out sleeping dancers. The rest of us were asleep in our seats, buried into pillows and blankets. Our legs rested on the stools in front of us or, on the subsequent more crowded buses, stretched straight up against the seat in front of us before folding into one twisted position after another. This quest for comfort, usually unfruitful, began at seven or eight o'clock in the morning and continued until the twenty-minute rest stop at eleven o'clock. The unwritten rule of absolute silence during morning hours provided precious catch-up sleep from the previous night.

My favorite rest stops were Howard Johnson's, the east coast chain of restaurants famed for twenty-eight flavors of ice cream and other family friendly fare. Crisscrossing the country we left a trail of the orange and turquoise trademark signs. Having them pop-up again along a highway, meant that we were on our way home. Most highways were two lane roads with no food service. We took detours into small towns—even smaller than the ones to which we were headed—where we ate homemade apple pie over which we experts often bestowed a five star rating. From coast to coast—before the advent of styrofoam—coffee tasted, unfailingly, like cardboard. Back on the bus, we read, talked, played cards, and wrote letters. (Transistor radios were new on the market and were expensive. None of us had one.)

We sewed elastic and ribbons on ballets slippers and pointe shoes. To prolong the life of pointe shoes, many of the women darned the tips with thick white (or pink if we could find it) darning thread. Most of us had watched our mothers mending the family's socks: back and forth and in and out. Even though toe shoes had little resemblance to my father and siblings' socks, darning was a tedious job that smacked of the domesticity I had been determined to avoid since childhood. Although it seemed as though the added thickness never added much additional use to the shoes, I continued darning through future bus tours. I certainly had the time. A more effective technique involved completely drying shoes after every performance. Radiators in our hotel rooms, if they were hot enough, served the purpose. Pouring shellac inside the box of the shoe was an even better way, albeit marginally, to preserve our shoes. I was careful to pour only a small amount of shellac so that it did not seep through the pink satin, leaving unattractive, yellow stains. This method worked best in our New York City apartments where we used kitchen ovens set at 200 degrees.

Pointe shoes were expensive and only principal dancers in major companies were given as many as they needed. Corps de ballet dancers were allotted the fewest pairs and small companies, such as the early Joffrey, gave out even fewer. Many of us bought additional shoes on our own. I was astounded when I learned that every New York City Ballet dancer, even those in the corps de ballet, were given as many shoes as she wanted. What luxury!

Arriving at our destinations at two or three o'clock in the afternoon, we usually pulled up in front of seedy but respectable hotels. Maria—my roommate on tour and in New York City (after Laurie left to dance in Europe)—and I worked efficiently so that one of us was always first in the hotel dining room. The other would drag in our suitcases and check-in. (Rollers were non-existent.) We had as long as two hours, as little as one hour, and, on occasion, even less before we would have to be back on the bus for the drive to the theater. I watched with pity as the one, or maybe two, waitresses became frazzled by a sudden influx of hungry and demanding dancers. Maria and I, first to be eating our meals of chopped sirloin steaks and boiled vegetables or chef salads, smugly congratulated each other on our timesaving strategy. As always, the evening's performance was only a few thoughts away.

Columbia Artists Management was a presenting organization that offered cities and towns a choice of classical vocal and instrumental soloists or us—the most expensive choice of all—a small dance company. All bookings were pre-sold. Traveling with the dancers were a ballet mistress, company manager, stage manager, wardrobe mistress, and, on the first bus tour, two pianists. By the second tour we had a music director and a six-piece orchestra. Bob insisted that his company perform with live music, an expense that most small dance companies were either reluctant or unable to incur. The intimacy and immediacy between music and dancers and performers and audience cannot be replicated with a sound system. This is true even with today's sophisticated equipment; it was most certainly true during the 1950s and 1960s.

Most of the country's municipal auditoriums were built during the WPA era in the 1930s and we performed in many of them. In an architectural style that could be called "Simple Art Deco," they were plain and colorless. The stodgy tan or gray wings and hand-pulled front curtain looked utilitarian. The wings, behind which dancers wait away from view before making entrances and to which they disappear after exits, were sometimes nonexistent. A single door on each side of the stage sufficed. Not quite the same magic is apt to be created when a ballerina has to float onto or off the stage via a door.

Some auditoriums did not have space enough behind the backdrop to allow our crossing unseen from one side of the stage to the other. When there was no crossover we would have to rehearse the entire program, changing our entrances to correlate with succeeding exits.

At one high school auditorium we used the basement gym for our crossovers. In rehearsal, running down a flight of stairs, across the gym floor, and up the other side was clocked at thirty seconds; time enough to make our next entrances. During the evening performance a high school basketball game was in progress. Another dancer and I, wearing short tutus and rhinestone tiaras had no time to waste. Our hard blocked pointe shoes clip-clopped on the gym floor as we dodged the players, leaving ten gangly teenage boys with their jaws dropped and a basketball to pick up.

At another high school auditorium stage, although there was room enough behind the backdrop for our crossovers, the backdrop itself became a problem. Instead of the usual one-piece curtain, three overlapping panels hung in place. Distinctly, if slightly, they quivered with each passing grand jump or turn. Did this backdrop represent a cost cutting measure? Had it been bought at a warehouse sale? Did a parent of a teen thespian own an upholstery business? There were many speculations after a skirmish with one of our soloists, a delicate Grace Kelly beauty.

She was turning: slow, traveling revolutions on the toes of one foot. Her other foot was held way up and away from her body, her long skirt orbiting around her. The turns rotated, unhurried, until her pink tipped right foot caught the edge of a panel. Suddenly she was swallowed up and disappeared. A few flails followed and then she emerged, still turning firmly on her left foot. The other foot seemed to remain chest height and, unbelievably, her movie star facade remained unflustered.

Sunday matinees were often booked into a town's old and only vaudeville/movie theater. Hooray! A real theater and located in the center of the town! We were one of few performing groups since vaudeville days to use the theaters and, surely, we were one of the last before they were redeveloped into other uses—such as furniture stores. The marquis might have read *Gidget Goes to the Beach* starring Annette Funicello and below it, "Today: Sunday Matinee 2:00 Robert Joffrey Theater Ballet."

Old theaters were often drafty, taking us a long time to warm up. We wore wool leg warmers, sweaters, and even scarves and gloves. Occasionally, if the stage manager had been delayed in setting up the stage, we did our barre in the lobby hanging onto a candy counter. The lobby smelled of rancid, buttered popcorn butter. The stage and backstage areas were filthy, and as tiny as the dressing rooms often were they were real dressing rooms with mirrors and lights; not big spare rooms or, most disappointingly, high school auditoriums and classrooms. Applying stage make-up and putting on pointe shoes in a classroom with blackboard assignments and wood desks carved with initials seemed amateurish. Real theaters were professional. The stages always had crossovers, heavy velvet wings, and dark, velvet front curtains. It never bothered me that the wings had hung there for decades and bumping into them sent columns of stage lit dust up into the rafters. We always danced our best in real theaters.

Most of our audiences had never seen ballet. We seemed, however, accessible, almost familiar. We were not a foreign company but an American company. Our ballets were nostalgic, cheerful, or gently dramatic and we performed each one with every bit of energy and love we could muster. Our audiences left with a spring in their step and autographs in their programs. It was important to Bob that we made good impressions off stage as well as on. All were welcome backstage to our dressing rooms for autographs. We donned our make-up robes and smiled at all the little girls and their mothers as they went from dressing room to dressing room or school desk to school desk. Some of us went beyond the call of duty and engaged the children in conversation. When they left, we stopped smiling and complained to one another about pointe shoes, the stage, or the next day's bus trip.

We dreaded after-performance receptions, usually hosted by well-meaning ladies' groups. We were tired, in need of showers, and hungry. There was no escape. The bus took us directly from the performance to our hosts' home. Ranch style houses with Danish modern furniture and silver plated trays laden with cream cheese finger sandwiches greeted us. Sometimes the cream cheese had been tinted with pink or green food coloring.

Soon after arriving, I would disappear into the guest half-bath to wash out the day's practice clothes. It was a pleasure to be able to use a large cake of pink Camay soap instead of the teensy soaps that the hotels of the day provided. Tights and leotards rolled back into my dance bag, I returned to polite talk, self-satisfied that I had gained an extra fifteen minutes of sleep for myself.

Muscle aches and exhaustion totally disappeared on those rare occasions when bountiful buffets awaited us. We descended upon the food with unrestrained glee. (Over forty years later, even without trying, I am still first in a buffet line.) We were happy to not eat the cottage cheese, yogurt, and fruit that we had stored on the window ledges of our hotel rooms.

Traveling became predictable with New England and its white church spires and winding streets; the South with hanging moss, magnolia trees, and signs that read "whites only;" the Midwest with main streets that stretched from hotel to planted fields; and the West with coastlines, mountains, and desert. Wherever we were, each day's schedule was the same as the previous one. It began on the bus, followed by hotel check-in, and on to the theater for class, rehearsal, and performance. Then, hopefully, back again to the hotel for a short night's sleep and not to a reception. Several times over the course of a one-night-stand tour, one of us would try to fit a room key in a lock from the room number of the previous night. After one such room entry attempt, a strange man's inquiring voice sent me scurrying away with supersonic speed.

I thought of hotel rooms as home. Although I would have preferred to spend more than one night in each home, I rather enjoyed how simple life was. I never seemed to need more than what was in my suitcase. Daily chores were condensed. There were no distractions. My focus was class, rehearsal, and performance—sometimes plodding, sometimes exciting, and occasionally adventuresome.

In retelling experiences from that first bus tour, all thirteen of us put the Eureka, California performance on top of the list. We had left Ukiah, California at seven o'clock in the morning for the one-hundred and seventy mile trip. Torrential rain had hit northern California and we had been warned that the roads were flooded and closed. We made a three-hundred and sixty mile detour going inland into Oregon through Grant's Pass in the Rocky Mountains along narrow winding roads and back down the coast to our destination. The bus did not have toilets. Having only four breaks, for both food and toilet necessities, was an additional challenge. At each of these stops, the company manager called ahead to Eureka with an update. Public payphones were the only means of communication. "We might be late." "We will be late." "We will be very, very late." The rain spilled out of the sky and, in the mountains, it turned into dense snow. Tiny, our three-hundred pound bus driver,

On stage in Niles, Michigan. (Left to right) Maria Grandy with Vincente Nebreda, the author with Alfonso Cata, Beatrice Tompkins with Gerald Arpino, and Francoise Martinet with Nels Jorgensen, in Todd Bolender's Whirligig, 1958. (photo credit: Richard Adelsperger/Niles Daily Star)

drove at his usual maniacal speed. His pride was on the line. Tiny had always gotten us to our destinations. (On another occasion, arriving late to Bartlesville, Oklahoma, Tiny took a shortcut by driving through the golf course at Fort Sill.)

After dark, six-foot snow embankments were lit along the road by the headlights as we rushed ahead. The windshield wipers scraped the snow as it accumulated against the wide windows. The sound of snow scrunching under the tires continued for hours. We stopped for a couple of extra minutes to allow the men to collect snow in paper cups. Melted, they used it to shave. We took out small mirrors and put on make-up. "The show must go on," we joked. It was rather thrilling.

When we reached Eureka, a police escort greeted us. It was ten o'clock at night. "Here they are!" I heard a woman shouting into the night from the door of the auditorium. Most of the audience had been waiting for two hours. We were bedraggled but we were in full stage make-up. They applauded as we came through the front of the auditorium, filed down the aisle to the stage and disappeared behind the curtain. In five minutes time, we had changed into practice clothes and were hanging onto our portable barres on stage. We did a shortened warm-up barre as our ballet mistress, Bea Tompkins (who also danced several principal roles), explained the reasons behind each exercise. After our warm-up it took only another five minutes to put on our costumes and be ready to begin. It was a record thirty minutes from bus to "Places please." And this from our young company that was generally in the theater from three to five hours before curtain time! In the future we performed for, arguably, more prestigious audiences, but in my heart none matched the one in Eureka, California.

We traveled with four short ballets, performing the same program each night. Even when the company expanded and toured with additional ballets we rarely had two completely different programs. Most of us (and all of us in the early bus tour days) danced in either three or all four ballets. Because we were so few, there were no unimportant roles and there were few, if any, understudies. Remarkably, there were few injuries. We danced with minor pains, colds, and fevers. Not dancing did not occur to us; it just was not an option.

Although dancing leading roles is more rewarding than dancing in the corps de ballet, dancers always try to dance to the best of their ability. Elated over a good performance and despondent over a bad one, most in an audience could not see a great difference between the two. There is always a level below which experienced dancers do not go. This does not alter a dancer's self-criticism, however. It can be harsh and no amount of praise can shake it. Just as unshakable is the certainty of having danced well.

Beyond dancing well, there are a few special performances, ones that keep dancers dancing. On those occasions, the mind, heart, and body soar effortlessly and the movement and music meld together. Transported, the dancer is both aware and unaware of her connection to the audience. No whisper or cough breaks the spell. And in the end there is applause. Intoxicating!

Maria—my Met Opera friend who had seen me through *Die Fledermaus*—and I shared gossip and giggles. We were particularly close with two of our partners: Vicente Nebrada from Venezuela (who would later direct the National Ballet of Caracas) and Alfonso Cata from Cuba (who would dance with New York City Ballet and found Ballet du Nord in France). Vicente gave everyone a cross gendered name. I was Paco Paquet. Not to be outdone, another dancer gave out saintly, if silly, names such as Sister Mary Merry and Sister Mary Martyr. Joining our foursome was tall, spindly, and irreverent Helio "Sonny" De Soto—a pianist Maria and I knew from taking classes from Igor Schwezoff, one of our favorite Russian teachers.

We were quite cosmopolitan for such a seemingly young and quintessential American company. A dancer whose parents had been born in Puerto Rico spoke Spanish with Vicente and Alfonso. She and her husband, a dancer and musician named John Wilson, joined the company midway. They had left their six-week-old daughter behind with a sister and grandmother. That would be the last time they would travel without their child. On this one the mother, Brunilda Ruiz, spent as many hours sobbing as she did dancing. Francoise Martinet and her mother, Manet, our wardrobe mistress, were French. Alfonso's family had lived in Paris where his father was a pre-revolution Cuban diplomat. Alfonso easily switched from speaking Spanish to French and back to English. (Upon retiring from performing, Francoise taught at the Joffrey School and the University of Iowa where she was instrumental in the university hosting two important Joffrey premieres: Robert Joffrey's *Nutcracker* and Gerald Arpino's *Billboards*, music by Prince).

Jonathon Watts, a soloist with New York City Ballet, also joined the company mid-way. As a guest artist, he danced Balanchine's "Nutcracker Pas de Deux" with Dianne Consoer. Jonathon and Dianne were in love; they held hands by day and danced by night. Other men in the company were Gayle Young (who would leave after the tour to join and become a principal dancer with American Ballet Theatre) and Nels Jorgensen (later, Director of the Louisville Ballet).

Lastly, Bob was fortunate in having a capable company manager. Jack Harpman took care of a myriad of details from soothing anger over—and compensating for—the ruined Fort Sill perfect golf course green to negotiating for more time to set up for a performance. If Bob was the heart of the company, Jack greased the gears.

By the second bus tour Maria would no longer be with the company and with her went the daily confidences of a dear friendship. My future husband, Paul, would join and together we would become committed to Bob and the Robert Joffrey Ballet.

Chapter 13

AMERICAN BALLET THEATRE

My dear friend Maria was not offered another contract; her weight had become a problem. A few years later she was again in the Joffrey fold as a teacher at the school. In the 1980s she was an assistant and then co-director of Joffrey II, a training company that had been established for the principal, larger Joffrey company.

Ballet dancers have always been thinner then their modern dance contemporaries. Generally, although less often today, modern dancers do not look like stereotypical dancers but often look like "girls next door." They can make a powerful impact by performing unexpected, extraordinary movements as well as performing ordinary movements in unusual ways. However, only lengthened, slim, stretched limbs and supple backs can accurately execute ballet movements. Ballet, an ephemeral art with an inflexible and demanding technique, can be both powerful and beautiful.

There are a few ballet dancers who become bone thin and bloodless looking. When I was dancing we never heard of eating disorders. I knew of only three dancers (all female) who had major problems with food. One was skinny with dull, thinning hair; the other went from plump to skinny and back again time and time again; and the third sucked the sugar out of cookies and then spit the pulp into a napkin. Lunch was a head of iceberg lettuce that she ate leaf by leaf, peeling it to its core as if it were an artichoke. At the time, we never thought of these dancers as unhealthy or sick, but merely odd and the subject of gossip.

Although I missed Maria, I would soon be spending time with Paul Sutherland, a former dancer with American Ballet Theatre (known as ABT or Ballet Theatre). We became inseparable and were soon talking about marriage.

On January 1, 1960, in the same living room where fourteen years previously at the age of eight my life had been irrevocably turned towards the stage, Paul and I were married. Just as that first dance in front of my parents had set their hopes for, and my certainty about, a successful career in ballet, this ceremonial performance inspired hopes and certainty for nuptial bliss.

Attended by immediate family and officiated by a minister who had uncommonly liberal credentials, the formalities were short of religiosity, suiting both the lapsed Catholics and church-adverse Protestants among us.

I surprised myself by being married as young as twenty-two. When a child, I had planned to wait until I was thirty before finding a husband, allowing ample time, or so I thought, for attaining ballerina status and its' attending fame and adulation. I would never have considered giving up dance for marriage, the accepted path for a young dancer in love in the 1950s and early 1960s.

Always fresh in my mind was the anguished face of a beautiful dancer struggling with the choice between a second year with Ballet Russe de Monte Carlo and the man she loved. I was thirteen years old and she was the first of my Boston teacher's students to be accepted into a ballet company. I could not understand her choice of domesticity over footlights and nor can I now.

However, marrying a dancer was different and marrying a dancer in the same company was ideal. Who else could understand how fully consumed I was with the giddy highs and heavyhearted lows of unrelenting work, struggle, satisfaction, disappointment, thoughts, and dreams?

Being married in 1960 had valuable advantages. It meant that my parents would never have to know that I had "lived in sin," I would not have to suffer severe frowns from hotel staffs (their disapproval could be as keenly felt as if they were family), and I would not have to look for a mate in my post dancing life.

There were, however, two main disadvantages of marriage. The first was its flip side, divorce. At least in middle-class Boston, divorce was a stigma, a failure, and the commencement of (erroneously, I would later learn) a pitiful life. There was a second and more immediate, pressing disadvantage. I took over household chores. It never occurred to me not to. Although fond of eating, I have never liked to cook. Now I was cooking for two and making the new bride/bad cook jokes that were in the lexicon of popular culture. And dishes! Neither I nor anyone else I knew had a dishwasher. Washing clothes meant hand wash or a trip to the Laundromat. Only if you were exceptionally lucky were machines located on the basement level of your apartment building and no one had the convenience of a front loader in her apartment. Cleaning, however, did not bother me, vacuuming always having been somewhat of a hobby.

"Good," Bob Joffrey said only partly joking when he heard that Paul and I were engaged, "stabilizes the company." We were the third couple in Bob's young company to get married. We first three couples all eventually divorced and following us there would be other married couples, some who would divorce and others who would not. This severely tested Bob's more hopeful than accurate assertion. I suspect that the percentage of divorces among dancers was the same as among non-dancers.

Not all married couples are paired on the stage, but Paul and I were cast as partners in much of the Joffrey repertoire. We looked good together both physically and stylistically. We were more or less on par with each other within the company hierarchy. We were always willing to go over that lift one more time, and we were never tired of analyzing scary balances (for me) and the even scarier turns (primarily for him). Off stage and at home we shared conversation, gossip, and intimate thoughts. Our relationship took over from the one I had with Maria, except that this one was closer.

Other married couples were not as lucky as we. If the man turned and jumped with the best but was short, had over developed thighs, and a perky, Peter Pan personality, he would probably never dance with his tall, leggy, and more regal wife. This was also true of the man who was tall (five feet, ten inches qualified as tall), had a great technique, and held the rank of soloist, but his wife, due to insecure technique and maybe too much weight on her hips, remained in the corps de ballet.

Two days after our wedding, we returned to New York, began rehearsals, and, after several weeks, we were back on tour.

Someone, somewhere along some mid-country highway, passed around a recent copy of *Dance Magazine*. Although all of us knew that ABT would soon be embarking on a six month European tour, this was the first time that any of us saw the full itinerary which included: Lisbon, Bordeaux, Brussels, Gothenburg, Zurich, Granada, Munich, Rome, Naples, Santander, Athens, etc. The list went on and on, leaving us all breathless. Alfonso, who had been everywhere, began describing the theater in Geneva, the canals of Amsterdam, and the Tivoli Gardens in Copenhagen. ABT would also be the first American ballet company to perform behind the Iron Curtain, with stops in Sofia, Bulgaria; Bucharest, Rumania; and Moscow, Leningrad, Kiev, and Tblisi in the Soviet Union.

"Imagine dancing in Leningrad," I said wistfully. St. Petersburg (as it is known now as well as before the revolution) was the holy grail of ballet. Pavlova, Nijinsky, *Swan Lake*, Tchaikovsky, and the Mariinsky Theater were names I knew from childhood. The Mariinsky Theater School and Company—renamed Kirov after the revolution, although the Mariinsky name continued to fall from dancers' lips— were among the best, if not the best, in the world. The ballet school auditioned hundreds of little boys and girls each year and accepted a handful. Once accepted, training was tuition-free.

By 1960, Soviet ballet companies had begun traveling to the West and their interpretations of the classics were unparalleled. Although American companies could not compete with *Swan Lake* and *Giselle*, they excelled in contemporary ballets. Even ballets choreographed as far back as the 1940s like Agnes de Mille's *Rodeo* was innovative to Soviet audiences. In the Soviet Union, contemporary ballets often had revolution-friendly themes. Dancers, high stepping across the stage in red toe shoes and carrying Soviet flags, looked ridiculous.

It had been rumored that Lucia Chase, Ballet Theatre's director, had been hiring married couples, apparently in reaction to the Soviet Union's well-known denials of homosexuality in their own ballet companies. The tour also coincided with an unusually long break between Bob's tours. The timing would have been perfect for our participation in this exciting tour. However, we knew that not only had ABT already hired all their dancers and that the company was in the fourth of a six-week rehearsal period, but also we were in Wyoming on our way to Los Angeles.

All Joffrey American tours, except this current one, ended in New York. Having been given money for airline tickets to New York, some dancers chose to stay on the west coast for a vacation. The rest of us returned to New York right away. The morning after we returned, the telephone rang. Would we be interested in joining Ballet Theatre? Could we come to the office immediately? With partially unpacked suitcases in the middle of the room and untouched mail still heaped on the table, we scrambled out the door.

"My, my," Lucia Chase said upon meeting me. "You do have a pretty face." Lucia was known to be partial to dancers with pretty faces. "Do you have nice feet?" ("Nice" feet mean attractively arched feet.) Lest it seem that Lucia, as everyone called her, was completely lax in her hiring practices, I guessed that ABT's ballet master, Fernand Nault, who knew me from classes and choreography at Bob's company, had spoken well of me. (In addition to Zachary Solov and Bob Joffrey, Fernand was someone without whom my life would have coursed through much more pedestrian paths.)

I assured Lucia that I had nice feet. What I did not tell her was that two days earlier I had broken my little toe. Throbbing painfully as we spoke, I did not know how I could manage the pain of wearing pointe shoes, but I knew that I would. No little toe—blue, bruised, or broken—was going to keep me from going on that tour.

I knew that dancing would be much easier than that of my Joffrey tours. American Ballet Theatre had ballets with large corps de ballets and I would be dancing only corps parts. Blending in with sylphs in *Les Sylphides* and cowgirls or housewives in *Billy the Kid* allowed me to make surreptitious, choreographic adjustments. Instead of doing a relevé (rise) onto pointe that would end with my weight, albeit for an instant, on my injured foot, I did a small sauté (jump) that prevented the dreaded pain associated with an otherwise, unremarkable step. A quick relevé and a sauté that barely rises off the floor looks pretty much like the same step among a large group of dancers.

How could I be clever enough to accommodate a broken toe and so stupid as to break it in the first place? It had happened in LA, the morning after the last performance of the tour. In my underwear and bare feet, I sang and danced and pranced around the hotel room. My tour-end celebration came to a shrieking halt as I completed a double pirouette. The carpet, acting like rosin, held my little toe in place while the rest of my body continued turning. A loud crack accompanied the pain. Weeks passed before I was comfortable enough to wear street shoes and months before I no longer needed to cut small holes in the sides of my pointe shoes. Using a razor, I cut through pink satin and layers of stiffened canvas. My little toe stuck out like a weird protrusion but it was somewhat pain-free. Joining the company after the rehearsal period worked to my advantage. Not being scheduled to dance until our first European stop in Lisbon, I had a few weeks before I needed to wear pointe shoes.

The tour was preceded by a New York season in a Broadway theater. I learned the ballets in which I would be dancing by watching from a sixth row, orchestra center seat. Under other circumstances, I would have been delighted with complementary tickets, but I was there to work. My job was to watch and transpose, mirror-like, the steps from the audience's to the performer's point of view. Written notes had to substitute for body memory. How I wished I had the ability, as did a few of my friends, to learn easily by observation alone.

Two days after the end of the New York season we departed from New York's Idlewild (Kennedy) International Airport. It had been only three years since my first tour, a Metropolitan Opera spring tour. At that time I was excited about traveling to Cleveland. Now I was boarding a chartered KLM plane bound for Lisbon. From my seat, I watched the propellers pick up speed until they were a blur. It would be a twelve-hour flight. Once aloft, stewardesses who were female, white, unmarried, young, and pretty catered to us. They had identical immobile smiles. Signs requiring passengers to keep seat belts fastened were lit only for take-offs and landings. We paced the aisles, changed seats, and talked, laughed, and shouted. Restrictions were few. We drank too much and smoked a lot. We were handed printed menus that included a personal welcome from KLM. On the back cover there was a list of everyone in the company. We were fifty-four dancers and seventeen staff. "I really am a dancer in a major ballet company," I thought.

It was early afternoon the following day when we landed in Lisbon. We popped out of our seats as soon as the wheels bumped onto the ground. All the women were uncomfortably dressed. None of us wore pants, nor, in 1960, did "leisure" suits or "sweats" exist. We wore skirts or dresses and we wore stockings. Pantyhose also did not exist; garter belts held up our stockings. Whether lacy and racy or cotton and functional, none stayed around our waists. Dragging down over our hips, they left pink creases in our skin.

The door of the plane opened and warm sun greeted us. The light hurt my eyes and my teeth felt fuzzy. Even though my feet were swollen and my toe was pressed painfully against my high-heeled shoes, I fairly danced off the plane and down the steps to the tarmac below.

Over the course of my career, I would participate in five foreign tours. This, the first, was the longest. Ultimately, there would be two more with ABT, a second to the Soviet Union and one to South America. With Bob's company I would go on yet another tour to the Soviet Union, as well as a tour to the Middle East and India. On every tour, company managers took care of all travel details, making our tours as free of distractions as possible. We walked through gates and past officials in snappy-looking caps. We never stood in line for customs, passport checks, luggage, or hotel check-in.

I was eager to begin rehearsals and actually dance in the ballets I had so arduously committed to memory. Whereas soloists need only be concerned about their own dancing, corps dancers need to be keenly aware of one another. They need to both dance in unison and move into precise stage patterns. Knowing that the ABT repertoire was much larger than that of the Joffrey and the dancers were more experienced, I did not expect the company to rehearse as compulsively as I had become accustomed. However, I did expect a "placement" rehearsal for each ballet. Held routinely in every theater, placement rehearsals, as the name suggests, is necessary to become accustomed to the size, shape, and depth of each new stage.

As expected, a placement rehearsal for *Les Sylphides* was called before the opening night at Lisbon's San Carlo Opera House. The stage, as were most on which we danced throughout our foreign tours, was raked (slanted), enabling the audience to more easily see sets and performers, hence, the source of the phrase, "to upstage." (An opera star, for instance, singing a love duet, might place himself slightly upstage and away from the audience and his beloved, forcing her to turn her back to the audience in order to face him—presumably, not her best angle.)

Of all the old European opera houses, including those of Peter the Great's Russia, the opera house in Lisbon, at thirty degrees, had the steepest rake. As corps dancers in *Sylphides*, our concern was bourrées (infinitesimal steps in a crossed fifth position, usually on pointe). With one arm daintily rounded over our heads, upper bodies slightly inclined and eyes downcast, our poses were identical. We practiced bourréeing both upstage and down as we maintained our straight or curving lines. Bourrées should look as though dancers are gliding, almost as though they are being lifted across the floor.

Achieving this goal with the stage's thirty-degree gravity challenge took a third of the rehearsal time. Traveling upstage we learned to lean into the movement while trying not to look as though our feet were chugging along behind us. Conversely, traveling downstage, we leaned back and kept our toes stepping as fast as possible to avoid falling forward into an unintended run or two.

Dimitri Romanoff, the company's regisseur (principal ballet master), began rehearsing the ballet from the beginning. I assumed that we would run through it to its end. We had hardly begun, when Dimitri stopped the pianist. "Not a good sign," I thought.

Dimitri Romanoff, along with Fernand, the company's second ballet master, rehearsed all of our ballets. Dimitri was born in Russia and moved to America in 1924. He was one of American Ballet Theatre's earliest dancers, having joined at its founding in 1940. As company regisseur, Dimitri had overall responsibility for how well the company performed. As a pupil of the *Les Sylphides* choreographer, Michel Fokine, he felt, perhaps, particularly answerable to the ghost of that great early twentieth century choreographer. Always ill-tempered while rehearsing the corps in *Sylphides*, Dimitri resorted to yelling as he obsessed over how we held our heads in the many poses we were required to strike. Tilted, turned, up or down, every nuance was only achieved by elongating the neck. This remained persistently elusive to a few of the dancers. How I wished for Fernand's more analytical and sympathetic touch!

Stopping and starting dashed my hopes of having a complete rehearsal. As a result I performed in my first *Sylphides* depending on my mental notes. "Right, left, left, right, left, right, right, etc.," I had memorized. The corps had short dances as well as many runs and bourrées, all of which finished in poses of two or four or more. There was no time to think about which knee or leg on which to alight. However, my memorized cues worked perfectly. Running with my sylvan sisters to the end of a musical phrase, I stopped and posed with confidence.

We did *Sylphides* at least once in every city beginning in May with the Lisbon performance. Four months later, we were dancing in Athens at the Roman Herode Atticus Theater, an amphitheater built in 450 A.D. Located below and a short distance from the Acropolis, marble columns, some standing and some in fragments, were strewn along the back of the stage. They were our backdrop.

Sylphides choreography, music, and costumes seemed to blend with the enigmatic surroundings.

Michel Fokine's 1905 choreography had no story line but suggested intangible dreams. Chopin's music, originally a piano suite, lent itself to the poetic reverie. Costumes were romantic tutus, distinguished from classical tutus by their length. Many layers of filmy white netting gathered at the waist, making the skirt puff out before flowing to mid-calf. Tiny clumps of blue flowers were sewn on the bodice.

Our hair was in a "classical," a style that is worn for the entire traditional ballet repertoire and passed on from dancer to dancer. A narrow ribbon (a shoelace was perfect) placed over the hairline, around the ears, and tied in back, provided an excellent base over which we pulled our hair over and around our ears. We then coiled our hair around and around into a flat tight bun at the back of our necks. A wide meshed hairnet—a staple at Woolworth Five and Dime—plus liberal use of hairspray and hairpins kept our hair lacquered in place. We placed wreaths of little blue flowers on top of our heads, the front of the wreaths just grazing the hairline of our foreheads. Around the wreaths, bobby pins were forced through the wire stems of the flowers. Next, the pins themselves were secured, each crossed with another. The resulting small steel X's scraped against our scalps.

After fixing our hair and applying make-up, we padded and taped sore spots on our feet and put on pointe shoes. We pulled on pink tights, stretching them up as far as we could to eliminate baggy knees and ankles. We safety-pinned wedding and engagement rings to the inside of our waistbands. Not remembering to fold the waistbands over at least once, risked having the prongs of a ring stick into our navels. Costumes had panties sewn into them and most dancers did not need bras. At last, we stepped into our costumes, fully prepared to be sylphs. On our backs were small, semi-transparent wings hastening us toward the stage, our rarified world.

At curtain time and after the lights had been turned off, we quickly and in character took our places on stage. There were no theater wings and the audience could see us gathered by the sides of the stage. This prevented us from doing last minute limbering kicks or stretches. Only a stealthy whispered, "merde," a dancer's wish for good luck, could be heard. Translated as "shit" in English from French, "merde" was, to us, an esoteric way of saying "good luck." It has been suggested that saying "merde" or "break a leg" recognizes and, thereby, eliminates a performer's fear of losing control. Dancers never ever say, "Break a leg."

In the semi-darkness, we sixteen sylphs took our places at the back of the stage and in front of the fallen columns. We made a semi-circle, with tall girls in the center and short girls at the ends. We all took the same pose, facing in towards the center. Standing on one leg, the foot of the other, like a pink satin arrow, pointed firmly into the floor just in front of the girl behind. Hands were daintily cupped close to the ear. All heads tilted perfectly to one side as though listening to a faint, maybe heavenly, sound. A delicate breeze went through the layers of netting, moving the skirts, cloud-like around our legs. The air brushed over our powdered necks, arms, and backs. It cooled our exercised legs.

We stood in our poses, waiting for the first strains of the violins. Not moving my head, I peered through the corners of my eyes and saw that the amphitheater's marble seats had been entirely filled. I lifted my eyes up beyond the highest row and saw the Acropolis in the middle distance. Even though I knew that the ancient temples would be lit, I was startled at what I saw. How stunningly elegant and starkly white the marble Greek columns were against the black sky! Holding my head still, I lifted my eyes above them into the empty night. A breath caught in my throat.

There, traveling in the Athenian sky on that September night in 1960, was the unmistakable point of light that was not a star. Moving at an even rate of speed, it made a wide arc over the Acropolis. It was Sputnik, the first and, up to that time, only satellite orbiting the earth. Sputnik was the Soviet coup that had so surprised and shocked the whole world.

For a moment I felt connected to both the past and future, but disconnected from the present. Then, stage lights gradually flooded us with a soft blue-white light and the first few chords of Chopin's music stirred us. We began to dance. Breathing and moving as one, I was, once again, very much connected to the present.

Our next performance of *Les Sylphides* would be behind the Iron Curtain, and three weeks prior to our performing it in the Soviet Union.

Chapter 14

USSR

"See the music. Hear the dance," Balanchine has often been quoted as saying. The ballets in which the choreography and music are so perfectly wedded that it is difficult to imagine their separation, were often the most exciting and satisfying to dance. I had the privilege to dance in four Balanchine ballets, *Pas de Dix, Allegro Brilliante, Square Dance* with Bob's company, and *Theme and Variations* with ABT. *Theme and Variations* or *Theme*, as it was abbreviated on rehearsal call sheets, was commissioned by ABT in 1947. Choreographed to music from Tchaikovsky Suite no. 3, it is cast with eight corps de ballet couples, four soloist couples, and one principal couple.

Theme begins with all the dancers on stage. Sixteen corps de ballet dancers form a wide V (open end towards the audience) and eight soloists form a smaller V in front of them. The two principal dancers stand closest to the footlights. The women's arms are held out to their sides just above their tutus. The men's arms are also held out to their sides but closer to their legs. All the dancers face in towards the center with their heads and eyes lifted and turned towards the audience.

Standing there, in fifth position, we were totally still and intensely alert. Arrested motion, our poses were never frozen. I can still hear the heavy curtain part as it rushed to the far sides of the stage. The conductor's baton lifted. The excitement built. With a barely imperceptible lift of the arms, head, and eyes, we took a deep breath. The front legs extended forward and pointed feet slid along the floor. The intricately patterned and musically precise *Theme* had begun. I felt as though I was a thread in a beautiful tapestry, a kaleidoscope of movement and sound.

In contrast, one swan more or less in *Swan Lake* did not make a substantial difference. Similarly, there are some musical pieces, like a Puccini opera, where the total number of musicians may vary and in others, like Arnold Schoenberg's *Verklaerte Nacht* for example, where the piece is scored for a precise number of players. (However, being one of sixteen or thirty-two long-necked swan creatures in a ballet that has called so many little girls to the stage was magical in its own way.)

Balanchine's choreography and stage patterns compel, pied piper-like, the dancers to dance. Just as in speaking a favorite poem with one word following inexorably after the other, the steps seem to spill one after another. And just as one is aware of the poem's individual word as well as the meaning of the whole, to dance in a Balanchine ballet was to simultaneously experience a part as well as the whole.

Another choreographer, whose ballets instilled the sense of the whole, was Antony Tudor. The sometimes caustic and feared teacher from my Metropolitan Opera Ballet days took particular care in rehearsing his own ballets.

Whereas Balanchine's ballets seemed brilliantly connected to the structure of the music, Tudor's ballets seemed inspired by the psychological underpinning of the music. *Dark Elegies* with music from Mahler's *Kindertotenlieder* (*Songs of Childhood Death*) is an example. In the early stages of teaching his ballets, Mr. Tudor did not use a rehearsal pianist, but hummed and sung the score. Eventually, we dancers began to hear, in our minds, our own voices. Our bodies as instruments joined by our internal voices seemed to enhance Tudor's less classical and more naturalistic movement style of his darker ballets.

More often than not, dancers learn ballets by counting to, at least some, of the music. After enough practice the counting drops away. It was while rehearsing with Mr. Tudor that we learned how not to let counting get in the way of responding to the quality of the music. Silently singing the counts as if they were lyrics, our imagined voices kept us both physically and emotionally connected to the music.

Mr. Tudor insisted that each step of his choreography be executed with deep concentration. Indeed, it could be just an ordinary walking step or a sudden spring into the air or a fall to the floor. The movement, Mr. Tudor insisted, should appear to grow from some unseen psychic source. Whenever *Dark Elegies* was performed no one was allowed to watch from the wings. Any possible distraction from our experiencing the intensity of the stark and spare movements was eliminated. It looked odd to see the wings empty.

The wings are where dancers watch friends, rivals, and the company's leading dancers. It is where parts and passages are understudied and critiqued. It is where dancers pause to take a moment's break on their way to some other back stage destination. Generally there are fewer entrances and exits from the wings closest to the audience, making it less busy. From this vantage point, most of the stage can be seen. We knew enough to not only stay out of the performers' way, but to remain unseen by any of the audience sitting at the extreme sides of the house.

Although three-month-long one-night-stand bus tours with the Joffrey Ballet seemed to stretch on forever, the five and one half month ABT tour to twenty-eight cities in Europe, Eastern Europe, and the Soviet Union passed by swiftly. The company learned to say "please," "thank you," "yes," and "no" in fifteen languages. Sign language filled in the gaps. In the days before calculators, we converted dollars into drachmas, escudos, or rubles with reasonable speed.

We were two months into our ABT tour and two months from our historic visit to the Soviet Union, when a major international incident rocked American-Soviet relations. Cultural exchanges had become the baby steps used to warm the cold war. The exchanges, including our visit, were in jeopardy. An American U2 spy plane had been shot down over Soviet territory on May Day. Referred to then and now in history books as the U2 incident, it would be a long time before the two countries returned to their former tepid relationship.

US pilot Gary Powers was arrested. President Eisenhower's denial that the U2 was a spy plane and his insistence that the plane was related to weather research sound ridiculous today. However, in 1960, I not only believed the President, but was shocked that our government would actually lie. The pilot, if he had survived the crash, was expected to have swallowed a suicide pill. Gary Powers survived and he did not swallow the pill. Ultimately, he would spend seven years in a Soviet prison before being released as part of a spy exchange.

My great concern, however, was not political but professional. Would we still be allowed to proceed to the land of Pavlova and Nijinsky? When, finally, we were told that the tour schedule would remain intact, we were relieved and happy. So, in October 1960, we boarded one of Aeroflot's fleet of jets. For most of us this would be our first time flying in a jet. The speed was amazing. "One one-thousand, two one-thousand, three, four, five and six," I counted. "We've gone one mile!" I announced periodically throughout the flight.

We loved the speed of our flight to Moscow, but were less than impressed with in-flight customer service. We had become accustomed to pushing the little call buttons above our seats and watching charming English speaking stewardesses—whose accents were always captivating—skim down the aisle to attend to our needs. Neither turbulence nor lack of sleep nor rude passengers could shake their unwavering good humor as they provided us with magazines and glasses of water.

Upon fastening our seat belts in Paris and in the air bound for Moscow we spoiled passengers knew that this flight was going to be different. Sturdy, unsmiling matrons who looked a though they may have posed with a tractor for an agricultural commune poster, charged down the aisle. Placing a tray of food on our laps, they said "Nyet," if anyone asked for butter or a soda. Sitting on our plates were boiled half chickens. They were tough. The skin was yellowish, cold, and wrinkled. They came with a roll. Somehow, we knew not to use the call button for any request except, perhaps, for an air-sickness bag.

Arriving in Moscow, snow was coating the runway. It was after dark. And there we were, seated in a jet-powered plane, Sputnik was circling the globe, and outside our windows the runway was being swept clear by six women bent over short-handled brooms and wearing padded jackets and babushkas.

The U2 incident did not delay customs or related paper work. In no time, we were bussed into the center of the city and booked into a gargantuan hotel built for foreigners. The building's architecture, dubbed Stalin Gothic, was formidable. It had neither the elegance of classical decoration nor the simplicity of a modernist style, but it did look imposing and functional. The lobby was cavernous. The only Russians we ever saw in the hotel were hotel workers and interpreters.

If there were shops selling sundries, postcards, and newspapers, I didn't find them. Neither did I see bellhops. The front desk staff did not take on concierge duties. Not only could they not locate the room number of one of our group, but also a request for a room number of someone other than our group, was met with an adamant "Nyet!" Withholding this information, I decided, was simply an example of the Soviet fondness for secrecy.

The hotel keys were overseen by what we dubbed the "Soviet Key Police." Large, serious women sat by the elevators on each floor. They handed you your key as you went to your room and retrieved it upon your leaving. No rendezvous with newfound Russian friends was possible under this system.

What a gleeful discovery it was that in a brand new hotel in Kiev, all of the keys worked in all of the doors! Amusingly, the Soviet Key Police remained as staunch as ever in their duties.

Before leaving America, we had been warned that our rooms would probably be equipped with listening devices. Our having decided that they were in the overhead lighting, many of us addressed the ceiling. "We have Howard Johnson's twenty-eight flavors of ice cream," I shouted. "Is chocolate, vanilla, and vanilla with raisins the best you can do?" "Your pear-flavored soda is disgusting." "Any fresh fruit in this city?" "Any chocolate in the chocolate bars?" And, delivering the unkindest cut of all, I continued, "Your scratchy toilet paper is the worst in the world." This was as political as my tirade got. I was careful not to mention anything that might get anyone in trouble.

We knew that the hotel maids skimmed the tops off bottles of French perfume, replacing it with rubbing alcohol. Although it was strictly forbidden for Russians to buy or foreigners to sell Western made products, some company members sold high demand items like stockings, high-heeled shoes, perfume, jeans, ties, and records. Polyester clothes, apparently not manufactured in the Soviet Union, were popular. Clothing labels were sought after. In 1960, showing off and valuing a brand name seemed bizarre.

The most risky transaction was exchanging dollars for rubles on the black market. Even though the rate of exchange was many times more favorable than that of the official rate, temptation was low. Rubles were worthless outside the Soviet Union and there was, after all, a limit as to how much amber jewelry and how many art books and hand painted lacquered boxes we could carry home in one suitcase. A few dancers, however, did use the black market and a few others bought and smuggled Russian icons out of the country. My only questionable activity was squirreling away a book of Chinese opera designs in with my make-up and leotards. Although it was not illegal to take the book out of the Soviet Union, it was illegal to bring anything made in China into the States.

There were a few young Russian risk takers who not only bought our jeans, but befriended us as well. Edward and his wife, Valia, hung around a street corner a block from our hotel waiting for someone from the company to walk by. Stopping Paul and me, they were eager to know if we knew Duke Ellington, if we owned Elvis Presley records, and if we had ever been to Hollywood. Edward's English was self-taught. Our conversations were stealthy. He had no interest in politics or the ballet, but both he and Valia were in love with American popular culture.

By the end of our week in Moscow, we promised to correspond and to mail them a shopping list of items they had pressed into our hands. It was only upon our return to the Soviet Union three years later in 1963, did we realize the great value of the many vinyl records we had sent. Edward had made tapes of them, still a rather new technology, and sold them. He made many Russian friends happy and made himself and Valia well off enough to bribe themselves to the top of a long waiting list for an apartment in one of the many buildings springing up just outside the city. By the time of our 1963 visit, restrictions against fraternization—a favorite Soviet word—had loosened considerably and we visited Edward and Valia in their new small one bedroom apartment. They were especially pleased that they did not have to share their apartment with any other family members. The tiny kitchen boasted a small refrigerator along with a closet full of whatever foodstuffs happened to be for sale. If there was a line outside a shop, one of the two of them got into it before even knowing what was being sold. A queue meant there was something worthwhile to buy. Knowing that an item might not be available again, our friends stocked up. At the time of our visit, they had twenty-five cans of mushrooms and, lined up on the floor, six pair of fashionable western-style women's shoes from Yugoslavia, none of which actually fit Valia but all of which would fit someone.

Our government hosts were intent on our not meeting people other than themselves and the several interpreters who traveled with us. The interpreters, all women, spoke excellent, nearly accent-free English. They were dedicated believers in the Soviet system and we engaged them in amiable arguments. They were gracious and friendly and they loved the ballet. I was especially fond of Tamara who seemed more interested in our lives as dancers than in talking about the Soviet Union.

In an effort to keep our free time busy and under a watchful eye, our hosts planned excursions—another favorite Soviet word. Tamara and the other interpreters could not understand why ABT management would not force us to attend each and every one.

We all turned up for the tours to the Hermitage, the Summer Palace, the Kremlin, and Red Square. We never had to stand in line. The longest one was at Lenin's tomb where people, bundled up from the cold, stared at us resentfully as we passed. Inside, we viewed Lenin's body, a strange experience. The only dead people I had ever seen were the recently deceased at funerals, not someone who had been mummified, mustache intact, and dead for decades. A religious, hushed quality hovered, making the experience seem even more macabre.

In Tblisi, Georgia, we were taken on a daylong excursion to a collective farm, an outing that became more unattractive the longer we drove. After a two-hour bumpy drive, we were far more interested in eating than seeing an agricultural commune. Just as well, since it became apparent that our farm tour consisted of a pass-through of an immaculate, small, typical worker's house. Standing silently was an old woman. Being as immaculate and spare as the house, she seemed almost inanimate except for her look of weary curiosity.

We waited for the feast that had been prepared for us; we were famished, a common cry among ballet dancers. Sitting along the sides of a long, wood table in the town's community room, we waited for the Georgian representative to finish his statistic sprinkled speech. Every sentence was translated first from his native Georgian tongue into Russian and then into English. Pronouncements of collective farm successes droned on and on. Finally, bowls of vegetables and fruits were set in the table. The one vegetarian dancer in the company, a rarity in 1960, teared up. Up to that point, Rosemary had only eaten tomatoes, potatoes, pale pink borscht, and bread. Brought next to the table were two roasted suckling pigs, possibly creating additional vegetarians among us.

After every few mouthfuls of food, someone would stand up and offer a toast to the "friendships of our two peoples." The long toasts of our hosts were little speeches. Translations made them even longer. We shoveled in as much food as we could before being required to stop, raise our glasses of vodka, and listen to the next toast.

A tea-packing factory excursion had been planned for later in the week. I sat that one out.

Ballet, of course, was our principal focus. We looked forward to observing demonstration classes at the Kirov Ballet School in Leningrad. Soviet dancers and companies had only begun to perform in the West. They stunned the ballet world with their virtuosity, grandeur, and beautiful port de bras (carriage of the arms). Russian dancers have long been famed for the use of their arms and upper bodies. Far from being merely graceful and well coordinated, Russian arms, especially those of the women, seem to begin not from the shoulders but from somewhere deep in the back. From there, they seem to stretch outwards beyond the fingertips into space. In addition, the arms coordinate so perfectly with the head, neck, eyes, and legs that every part of the body seems to extend and breathe with every movement, large or small. Think of international figure skating competitions and recall the dance quality of the Russian skaters.

Many more dancers today have beautiful port de bras, but my early training, as well as that of many of my contemporaries, was primarily focused on legs. The arms were often taught as an afterthought.

What a morning it was when we were bussed (we were always bussed even if our destination was within walking distance) to the classroom studios in the Kirov Theater! Beginning with seven-year old boys and girls in their first year of study and finishing with teenagers in their final year, we were among the first dancers in the West to glimpse into the training behind the extraordinary Russian dancers. Today, after decades of exchanging dancers, teachers, choreographers, and companies, Russian dancers are not as unusual as they once were, but in 1960 they were astounding. I marveled at the height and speed of the men's leaps and turns, as well as their strength as they lifted and vaulted their ballerinas into and through the air. I marveled at the women's meticulous execution of each step and their fearlessness during each partnered toss and lift.

Looking like little adults, the seven-year old boys in their white undershirt tops, black trunks, and black ballet shoes and the girls in their white tunics and pink ballet slippers with braids tightly wound and flat on their heads, executed their short class perfectly. Their little legs, still more skinny than muscled, were mottled pink from the cold studio. All the studios seemed to be cold. In this, the first year of study, the children learned only a few steps that they repeated until perfect. They had classes every day. In my first years of study, I had one class a week and I learned many steps, necessitating many years to perfect them.

Reciprocating, American Ballet Theatre invited teachers and advanced students to watch one of our company classes. Our ballet master, Fernand Nault, first joined ABT in 1944. Upon retiring from dancing in the mid 1950s, he became the company's ballet master charged with giving classes, rehearsing, and coaching. His sparkling French Canadian eyes and humor never failed to lift our spirits, no matter how tired we might have been. Fernand, wanting us to make as good impression as possible, hand picked the company members for the class that day. All of the soloists, but not all of the corps de ballet were chosen. I was one of the chosen members of the corps.

It can be unnerving to have an audience watch class. It is in class where teachers either push dancers' limits or where dancers may take it easy, concentrating only on warming up for rehearsal or performance. Having an audience automatically meant that the class would be presented and viewed as a class/performance. We danced in one of the Kirov studios that had a floor raked to the same degree as that of the stage. Although we had already learned to adjust our repertoire to raked stages, steps and combinations of steps are, for corps dancers in particular, vastly more difficult and complex in class.

Dancers who train for years to execute both fine and bravura choreography and then suddenly face a slant in a floor are challenged, so to speak, at every turn. Being used to leaning slightly forward, for example, would be too far forward on a slanted surface, resulting in "missed" turns, and off balance finishes.

Fernand, with his usual enthusiasm, taught a well-prepared and "dancey" class, a class that had a musical kind of flow. (Some teachers give steps that follow one after another, almost like a choppy list.) I am sure that Fernand made us look as good as possible. We were reasonably satisfied with ourselves. The Russians were polite, if not enthusiastic.

We began our tour of the Soviet Union in Moscow at the Stanislavsky Theater for three performances, and then in Tblisli at the Opera House, followed by Leningrad at the Cultural Center. I would have to wait for the Joffrey tour in 1963 to step onto the legendary Kirov stage, or the Mariinsky as it was known before the revolution. The ABT tour continued at the Palace of Culture in Kiev, and finally, back to Moscow for nearly a week at the Luzhniki Sports Palace. The Sports Palace was sold out and people were turned away. Russians loved ballet and they were curious about American ballet and American dancers. Ballet, opera, and symphony were popular and tickets were inexpensive. In addition, there was little competition in the way of popular entertainment.

We performed George Balanchine's *Theme and Variations* at least twice in each city. Balanchine was born in Georgia in 1905 and trained in St. Petersburg.

Immigrating to Paris before the revolution, he had become a world-renowned choreographer. He and his New York City Ballet are, for many, synonymous with American ballet. Perhaps the Soviet Union was neither happy about acknowledging a famous expatriate nor in appreciating his progressive, avant-garde choreography. The critics even greeted the neo classical *Theme and Variations* with faint praise.

On opening night in the Stanislovsky Theater, Nikita Khrushchev was in the audience. During curtain calls, I looked up at the stage left mezzanine box to get a glimpse of him. Reviews for this Moscow performance, as well as those during the rest of the tour, were guardedly favorable.

All of our audiences, however, were wildly enthusiastic. Frenzied applause and shouts of "bravo" followed each performance. I had only heard such enthusiasm from Metropolitan Opera audiences—audiences that held Maria Callas, Renata Tebaldi, Jussi Bjorling, and Leonard Warren in adulation. As thrilling as those ovations were, I didn't identify with opera stars the way I did with the stars of ABT: Maria Tallchief, Igor Youskevitch, and Eric Bruhn.

If I were destined to be a star, I knew exactly how I would thank my audience. For years, at the end of class, many teachers would choreograph a grand and elegant reverance. Sometimes, the teacher would instruct the pianist to play while we improvised. Of course, on stage there was no music during curtain calls, but by practicing with music we learned to linger over each flourish. I was curtain call ready.

Curtain calls for those who are not principal dancers, however, are modest affairs. Men and women stand on their right legs. The women point their pink, toe-shoe clad feet behind the backs of their right ankles. The men, wearing either black or white soft ballet slippers, plant the balls of their back feet. Dancers take curtain calls like they dance; feet, knees, and hips are turned a full forty-five degrees outward from their bodies.

Companies rehearse curtain calls. The format may vary slightly. Standing in a straight line, corps dancers run forward. In a contemporary piece they might also hold hands. After a quick bow in unison, they run backwards, leaving room for the soloists to run forward. The applause swells. The principal dancers, waiting in the wings, let a few seconds pass before making their entrance. Running at a more measured pace, they go center stage. The ballerina stands slightly in front of her partner and they both bend and gesture in glory. The curtain closes and opens again. Sweeping her arm above the orchestra pit, the ballerina acknowledges the conductor and musicians. The applause swells again. For special premieres and ballets which feature solo musicians, the ballerina graciously leads the conductor, musicians, and choreographer from the wings onto the stage to stand beside her and her partner. The musicians often look awkward and uncomfortable as they move downstage alongside of the dancers. Curtain closes.

Final bows may be taken in front of the curtain. A stagehand separates the curtains from the center and, holding one of them, steps back leaving a corridor of space through which the principal dancers file out in front of the curtain. The curtain is kept parted just wide enough for the stagehand to see when it is time to widen it again for the dancers' return. It is in this moment when one might see a minor mishap like telltale knuckles against the dark velvet of the curtain, a stagehand carrying scenery, or a corps dancer scurrying out of eyeshot. We corps dancers, accurately gauging the energy of the continuing applause, would either hurry along to our dressing rooms or dawdle backstage prepared to respond to the command, "Full company!"

Russian audiences called us back many times. Additionally, the principal dancers were showered with special appreciation by a shift from clapping to a loud rhythmic clap. Growing ever louder, it sounded like a thunderous chant. The entire company was treated with this sound at our final Moscow performance, the last of our 1960 ABT tour. We had twenty-three curtain calls. We were bowing for forty-five minutes.

The next day we were on our way home.

Chapter 15

BACK TO BOB

Back in New York, Paul and I unpacked our suitcases, picked up mail from the post office, and restocked the refrigerator. We were anxious to see Bob and begin taking his classes.

The next day we climbed the stairs to the Joffrey studio, greeted old friends, and took our places along the barre. Bob entered the studio with a big smile. "I'm surprised that you came back," he said. "What?" I was shocked at his surprise. Didn't he know that we joined Ballet Theatre on the condition that we were allowed to sign a six-month only contract, not a full year as was required of nearly everyone else? Did he not believe us when we told him that we would return? Didn't he know that we were dedicated to becoming the best possible dancers and we needed his guidance? Bob had been heard to say, "I train them and then they leave." Not us. We gave Bob almost guru-like status. Of course we returned.

By 1960, the Joffrey School and company headquarters had moved to 434 Sixth Avenue in the village, where the school is still located. Bob and Jerry Arpino no longer lived in a room adjacent to the studio, but rented a nearby McDougal Street apartment.

Additional dancers had been hired. They called Bob, Mr. Joffrey, which sounded stiff and strange. We older dancers continued calling him "Bob." This never lessened our respect for him; it was an acknowledgment of a personal, teacher-coach/dancer bond.

Among the new dancers in the company were: Sara Leland, who would soon leave for New York City Ballet and rise to principal status; Gage Bush, who left for American Ballet Theatre and, upon retirement, co-directed Ballet Theatre II (a junior training company); Rochelle Zide, who had come from Ballets Russe, and would reconstruct and teach ballets world-wide; and Eleanor D'Antuono, also from Ballet Russe.

Eleanor had been the young talent who had so unnerved me during my junior high school performance. Remaining with Bob for only six months before joining

American Ballet Theatre, Eleanor rose to ballerina status and performed, among other ballets, *Swan Lake*. (In the book *Ballet and Modern Dance* there is photograph taken in the late 1960s with Eleanor as the Swan Queen and me as one of the corps of swans. In another supporting role, I was her matron of honor at her wedding.)

Nels Jorgensen with the author, in Robert Joffrey's Pas de Deesses, *circa 1961. (photo credit: Zachary Freyman)*

Many of these new company members seemed to have supreme self-confidence, often in short supply, along a ballet barre. Whereas most of us while taking class or rehearsing stopped to fix a turn that was off balance, others garnered the last bits of momentum to pull themselves around for one extra turn, not only finishing but finishing upright.

I marveled at the dancers who learned quickly, but was annoyed at the choreographers who then instructed the rest of us to execute a phrase in their manner and timing. "Damn," I would think. While I held back until I was sure of being precise, the dancer who completed the phrase first was the one to whom the choreographer was drawn. And there we were, the rest of us, told to follow along behind. "Damn," I would think again.

Unquestionably, it was Lisa Bradley (Bob changed her name from Rita) who would most impact the company. Still a teenager, she was blond with a delicate face and milky, blue-white skin. She was bird-boned and flexible to the extreme. Only her innate good taste prevented her from looking like a contortionist. Taking a step or pose up to that point gave her an edge the rest of us did not have. Her highly arched feet seemed to descend, weightlessly, on clouds.

Extremely flexible bodies, though beautiful, can be weak. A high leg extension can hinder a leap if the legs and back are not able to push strongly enough off the floor. And an extremely high instep can thwart a turn if the ankles are not strong enough to rise and hold the turning position.

Lisa began training at thirteen and did not begin serious study until four years later. This was a very late start. Beginning classes are recommended for children by seven, eight, or, at the latest, nine years of age and Lisa would struggle for strength throughout her career. Bob worked very hard with her. He gave her private lessons and pushed her into the more difficult corps roles to challenge her technique. Both Bob and Jerry began choreographing ballets for her. With each successive tour, it became clear that Lisa was the major inspiration for both men. "This is not fair," I thought. The rest of us have to prove ourselves before stepping ahead and Lisa has roles tailor-made for her body. If she can't do a step, it gets changed. But Lisa had an undeniable presence and an instinctive sense of drama. As delicate as she appeared, her style could be powerful and she was always compelling to watch. Although Lisa's being a favorite created angst among the female dancers, there were many roles to go around and I was busy with my share.

Today, all dancers seem to have slim, perfectly proportioned, and extraordinarily flexible bodies along with strong and impressive techniques. With the exception of a few ABT dancers and a greater number in New York City Ballet, neither my colleagues nor I would have been able to stand up against today's dancers. None of us would be hired by ABT, The Joffrey Ballet, or, in all likelihood, the Met Opera Ballet or a host of other companies.

Interestingly, I hear said about dancers of today what I heard about my generation of dancers. "Dancers only care about a strong technique and how many pirouettes they can do. They use technique as an end in itself, not as a tool. They have no artistry." Today I also hear the complaint that there are no great ballet stars. Well, yes and no.

Dancers have and will always be concerned with their pirouettes. (A diary, from my early teens, records every occasional multiple turn I did, with ecstatic exclamation points.) And although there no longer seem to be many internationally renowned and celebrated dancers who are generally regarded as stars, I not only see superior technique but also artistry in abundance.

Over the last forty years, ballet companies have cropped up all across the country. As a result, there are many more retired dancers who teach. Generally speaking, each successive generation of teachers and dancers is more proficient than the last. Catching lumpy bodies, bent knees, and dangling feet in film and photographs in the early twentieth century became less likely mid-century and today, almost never. For the most part, however, the best available dancers have always filled dance companies. Truly, we stand on each other's shoulders. I appreciate the love and hard work of all who went before me, bent knees and all, and I hope that we of the 1950s and 1960s are similarly appreciated in spite of the occasional errant foot and much more modest technique.

Some contemporary choreographers have responded to the abundant strength and flexibility in their dancers by challenging the limits of the body as never before. Movements, jumps, turns, and lifts are reinvented: legs stretch beyond ninety degrees; backbends fold in half; six and more revolutions are commonplace; and speed and stamina can take an audience's breath away. In such extreme choreography, it is the choreographers who are in danger of using dancers' capabilities as an end and not of service to the music or story line or idea.

Choreography requiring the dancers to perform one demanding feat after another without, seemingly, any context can be monotonous. After such a ballet, I am not only not lifted, moved, thought-provoked, or inspired, but also I can barely pull myself out of a stupor to applaud the sweaty, hardworking dancers.

One choreographer, who uses dancers to the extreme and, through it, has created what has been considered a masterpiece is Twyla Tharp's *In the Upper Room*. Using a commissioned Philip Glass score, the ballet has speed, energy, context, contrast, musicality, and innovation. Each movement fits meaningfully

Nels Jorgensen with the author, in Lew Christensen's Con Amore, *circa 1961. (photo credit: Zachary Freyman)*

into the next and watching it, I never want it end. Interestingly, Twyla Tharp's background is modern dance.

Dancers flourish with good work. Performers who dance a role both expressively and skillfully will impart something intangible, something eloquent, poignant, powerful, or compelling. I believe the reason there are fewer dancers that can be universally acknowledged as having this artistry is precisely because there are so many more of them, in so many more companies, in so many more cities.

Currently many companies list dancers alphabetically, eschewing the old star system that depended on the few to bring in the public. Even though some large classical companies separate the principal dancers from the soloists and corps de ballet, they, too, are listed alphabetically. It seems to me that it is the companies and their choreographers that have taken on the starring roles.

I am grateful that I had a ballet body that was good enough, a technique that was good enough, and opportunities to perform roles I loved. One of my favorite roles was that of Grahn in *Pas de Deesses*. Choreographed by Bob, it was danced, during my first year in the company, by Dianne Consoer before she left to join New York City Ballet.

Injury is not a dancer's sole opportunity to perform an understudy part. Sometimes company directors will give an understudy performance experience by scheduling her at a matinee, more often than not, in a small town. Most dancers are gracious to their understudies. Small details pertaining to both technique and timing can be very helpful. And a friendly face watching in the wings is a comfort; seeing a less than helpful dancer watching from the wings is not.

Bob scheduled my first performance of *Pas de Deesses* in Northhampton, Massachusetts, a college town not far from Boston. My parents, brother, sister, and my favorite aunt and uncle were in the audience. After the performance, effusive compliments and congratulations from my family and restrained but more valued ones from Bob surrounded me.

I saw my mother walk over to Dianne, who was standing on the sidelines. Dianne smiled and said, "You're welcome." My mother was thanking her for her letting me do the role. "Should I have thanked Dianne?" I wondered briefly. But then, I reminded myself, my doing the role was Bob's decision, not hers. I did not thank her and was a little annoyed that my mother had.

Before long, Dianne left the company and Grahn was my role; no one else would do it for as long as I remained with the company. The pang of watching an understudy do one of my parts came with another ballet, *Con Amore*. After many performances dancing the part of the Mistress, Bob scheduled my understudy much the same way as he had once scheduled me to do Grahn. When my understudy thanked me for letting her do the part, I learned that a simple "thank you" makes an inevitable loosening of the knot of role ownership easier.

Con Amore, choreographed for San Francisco Ballet in 1953 by Lew Christensen to Benjamin Britten's arrangement of three Rossini Overtures, was a light comic ballet that made a good program finale. In the first scene, Amazon

Warriors, led by their Queen, wore calf length ballet skirts and pointe shoes. Brandishing wooden swords, they did battle with the handsome Thief. The second scene opened with the Master bidding a fond farewell to his frothy, pretty Mistress, costumed in a filmy, pink negligee. Upon his leaving, a stream of suitors came calling. The third scene goes from nonsense to chaos: Amazons chase suitors, the Master embraces the Queen, and the Thief goes after the Mistress. Not a moment too soon, Cupid enters and with a gorgeous arabesque and a pluck on her bow, all gets sorted out. This was not the stuff of greatness, but fun all the same.

And never was it more fun than the last performance of one of the American tours. There is a show business tradition of performers playing little tricks on one another to celebrate the ending of a tour or stage run. Designed to "break up" colleagues into fits of laughter while keeping the audience unaware, antics from the imaginations of already naturally creative people are limitless. I have heard of everything from giving wrong cues to blackening front teeth. Such frivolity is rare in the ballet world, rarer in a small company, and unheard of in the Joffrey Ballet. But on one bus tour, just as the entire *Con Amore* cast was lined up couple by couple for the finale, one of us began to giggle. Along the back of the stage, walking slowly across was a second Student. It was Bob in a Student costume. None of us knew there was more than one; a pale-blue, prim, private school style uniform. As one of the Mistress's suitors, the real Student had overcome his shyness and was now embracing one of the Amazons, his part of the final pose. And there was Bob, nose in a book, behind us, making Joffrey Company folklore with each step.

It was clear that during the first rehearsals, Bob had someone else in mind for the Mistress. I knew that I would be the best choice for this quickly paced and quirky role, but how could Bob know that? Good comic timing was not part and parcel of the moonlight and roses parts in which I was usually cast.

One day, instead of stretching and chatting before class, I waited for Bob to leave his dressing room and stopped him. As I made my furtive plea, mild surprise crossed his face. Blocking his way, I continued talking until he said, "Ok, you can learn it." In the next rehearsal I learned the part. I was good in it, as I knew I would be, and before long I was in the first cast. (Early in the rehearsing process it is not unusual for the casting to change.) I found it satisfying to dance two contrasting ballets, *Con Amore* and *Pas de Deesses* on the same program.

Pas de Deesses (*Dance of the Goddesses*) had been inspired by an 1846 lithograph of Marie Taglioni, Fanny Cerrito, Lucille Grahn, and Arthur Saint-Leon. Bob, in capturing the tender qualities of ballet's Romantic Era, never stopped tinkering with a hand gesture here and the placement of a foot there. He used the music of

In Rehearsal: Joffrey Ballet Studios at 434 Sixth Avenue, 1962

(Left to right) The author, unknown, Mary Ellen Jackson, and Anna Marie Longtin. (From the collection of Marie Paquet-Nesson)

(Left to right) Lawrence Rhodes, Mary Ellen Jackson, Nels Jorgensen, and Gerald Arpino. (From the collection of Marie Paquet-Nesson)

In Rehearsal: Joffrey Ballet Studios at 434 Sixth Avenue, 1962

(Left to right) Carolyn Borys and Brunilda Ruiz. (From the collection of Marie Paquet-Nesson)

(Left to right) Paul Sutherland, James De Bolt, Lawrence Rhodes, and Gerald Arpino. (From the collection of Marie Paquet-Nesson)

John Field, a little known eighteenth century Irish composer whose music, it is said, inspired Chopin. The plot-less ballet opened on a pose that could have been lifted from the artist's lithograph. Each of the ballerinas took turns dancing a solo and a pas de deux. The male dancer gallantly partnered all three ballerinas before performing his own solo. The gentle rivalry between the ballerinas inspired even greater gallantry from their partner by his declining to choose a favorite. The ballet ended as it began, in the same carefully crafted pose.

For Grahn's solo variation, Bob choreographed swift and airy jumps and turns. Dancing the variation felt like being blown across the stage by a puff of wind from one of those Baroque zephyrs that were so often painted into cloud-filled canvases. Grahn's pas de deux was hugely strenuous for the partner. It included many lifts that had no preparatory jump and, therefore, no momentum, resulting in my being picked up as dead weight. Even a small preparatory jump would have marred the illusion of Grahn's floating weightlessly and effortlessly into and through the air. Thankfully, I had a very strong partner allowing me to enjoy another, more leisurely, current from zephyr's perch. The pas de deux ended with my being lifted and carried high into the wings. As I felt my partner's hands press into my waist and slowly push me upwards, my body settled into a deep backbend, my neck lengthening and resting as though on a pillow of air. As my arms and hands trailed behind me, I listened closely. A several second delay in the audience's applause would mean that the illusion we had created was, indeed, magical.

It was after such a performance that Bob would give me one of his rare compliments. Imparted between the two of us, in the shadow of a backstage prop or in a stairwell on the way to the dressing rooms, it felt as though he wanted no one else to hear. "Very good," he would say, or "That is the best I have seen you dance," or once or twice, "Excellent." When the usual intensity of Bob's small, dark eyes softened and shone as he spoke, these words became high praise indeed. One such treasured moment happened after a performance in Iran.

Chapter 16

THE MIDDLE EAST

The Joffrey Middle East tour began in December 1962 with a week in Lisbon. The tour, along with a Soviet Union tour scheduled for October 1963, was made possible in conjunction with the State Department and by the recent sponsorship of the Rebekah W. Harkness Foundation. Mrs. Harkness, widow of Standard Oil Corporation heir William Hale Harkness, was a woman of not only considerable wealth but also of considerable interest in the arts, ballet in particular.

In November 1962, one week before the start of the tour, we presented a thirty-minute program at the United Nations in the auditorium of the United States. Taking taxis to the United Nations Building for such a short program seemed less like a performance and more like a break between rehearsals.

We were featured at a reception hosted by the United States Representative Adlai E. Stevenson for the delegates to the General Assembly. The program read: "This (Cultural Presentations) Program, which is administered by the American National Theatre and Academy, will send the Robert Joffrey Ballet to the following countries: Portugal, Jordan, Lebanon, Syria, Afghanistan, Iran, and India." I was excited to meet Adlai Stevenson, who had been the Democratic Presidential candidate in 1952 and 1956. Several friends and I admired his intellect and humor. (When called an egghead, he said, "Eggheads of the world unite; you have nothing to lose but your yolks.") After the performance, I bounced over to him and announced, "My friends and I call ourselves, 'Daughters of Stevenson.'" "Daughters?" he asked, "Do I look that old?" Sixty-two looked old to me. He said that he enjoyed the program.

Among the short pieces we danced were two dances from *Dreams of Glory*, music by Mrs. Harkness. Beyond promoting and sponsoring dance, Mrs. Harkness was keen on fulfilling her own artistic ambitions. Having been trained as a composer, she had ballets choreographed to two of her earlier scores, each performed by a small European company. Her third score, *Dreams of Glory*, had been earmarked for us. The first payment for this piper's tune would be due in

Robert Joffrey pointing to a company poster in Kabul, Afghanistan, 1962. (From the collection of Dianne Consoer-Leech)

Lisbon, although not paid in full until Kabul, Afghanistan, Anver Abdullah Jaffa Khan's (Robert Joffrey) ancestral home.

The ballet, called *Dreams of Glory*, was in its second of three incarnations, each marginally better than the next. Choreographed in a workshop setting, which by definition implies experimentation, we hoped that *Dreams* would never see the light of day. We knew that this was a feeble hope since it was rumored that Mrs. Harkness liked the ballet and she was prepared to spare no expense for sets, costumes, and lighting. I presume that the choreographer was responsible for the story line. The original version was a tale of two children who, after watching a television newscast, daydream about being President and Mrs. Kennedy. The choreographer, Donald Saddler, was a former American Ballet Theatre dancer and an experienced Broadway choreographer. In his defense, the Harkness music did not leave much with which to work.

The ballet began with two children (played by Lisa Bradley and Larry Rhodes) watching the news on television, itself an unlikely scenario. Their mother, shaking her finger in irritation, bourréed towards them and, striking a penchée arabesque, reached for the knob and turned the television off. (An arabesque is a position with one leg lifted in back. In a penchée arabesque, the body leans forward so that the back leg is well above waist high.) The children began their daydream. Snippets, representing a day in the life of the President, included a dancer approaching President Kennedy in a medal ceremony. The dancer, Helgi Tomasson—who would ultimately be a principal dancer with New York City Ballet and, later, Director of The San Francisco Ballet—careened stiffly across the stage. Dressed in an astronaut costume and helmet he feigned disorientation, presumably because of recent weightlessness in space. Another medal was awarded to an Olympic swimmer. She wore a simple tank style leotard and ran, on pointe, arms rotating with champion style breaststrokes. Upon reaching the President, she stopped and pounded the side of her head, this time presumably, because of water in her ears. As the ballet progressed, the bad taste increased. Lisa and Larry Rhodes—who later became artistic director of Les Grand Ballets Canadiene before becoming Director of Dance at Julliard—tossed a doll that represented the young Caroline Kennedy in their dreams of glory. Back and forth between them the young Caroline went until the President was called away for a cabinet meeting, where he and his illustrious Secretaries tossed a beach ball, representing the globe, from one to the other. The very thought of performing this ballet for any audience, let alone one on a cultural exchange program, was deeply mortifying.

The death of this, the first version of *Dreams of Glory*, followed closely on the heels of the first run-through rehearsal. It was decided that the Kennedy theme was too personal and something more generic would be appropriate. Hence, a well-timed reincarnation came quickly to life. In the second version, the children's daydream was sparked in a portrait art museum by paintings of George and Martha Washington. An officious gallery guide replaced the mother and by eliminating contemporary snippets, the ballet easily slipped back two hundred years to George and Martha. As luck would have it, much of the choreography was deemed suitable to both the eighteenth and twentieth centuries.

In each of the two versions, Paul, another female dancer, and I performed the "Pas de Trios." A patriotic special, we were dressed in red, white, and blue. Paul's military blue jacket had shiny brass buttons and my friend and I wore short, classical tutus. My tiara headpiece was blazing with stars that poked up several inches above my head. The other tiara, more ugly than my own, had spikes resembling the crown of the Statue of Liberty. The "Pas de Trois" had been one of the segments from the ballet that had been chosen for the United Nations. As one of the few segments that did not cause embarrassment, it passed muster and the company danced that as well as the rest of the program without a hitch. One week after the United Nations inaugural performance we were in Lisbon preparing for the first full performance of *Dreams.*

The dress rehearsal was a series of disasters from entangling parts of costumes to the globe (ball) falling into the orchestra pit. (Yes, the globe—minus the Cabinet Secretaries—made a reappearance.) The entangled costume parts were a sleeve on Paul's costume with one of my wiry tiara stars. One of my friends still laughs as she remembers how, after tugging free from Paul's costume, I faced away from the auditorium (and Bob) to hiss expletives towards the back curtain. How many more mishaps would occur before Bob calls a halt to the performance, we asked ourselves? As we were to find out, not too many more. What a relief it was to see Bob charge down the aisle, yelling "Stop!" The first performance of *Dreams* would not be that evening, not in Lisbon. "If anyone asks," Bob told us, "Say the costumes were not ready." Since seamstresses hired from the San Carlos Opera House were still sewing on some finishing touches, this was partly true.

(The State Department had booked us in Lisbon to replace a Martha Graham cancellation. Even though the Portuguese dance community had been disappointed at not seeing the icon of modern dance, we won them over, although maybe not as easily if our curtain had opened onto *Dreams.*)

The first performance of *Dreams* was now scheduled for Kabul. It was nice to know that the likelihood of a dance critic residing and working anywhere in Afghanistan was remote.

Fifty costumes and many sets arrived in Kabul. By a surprising stroke of good sense, there were no hooped skirts or white powdered wigs in this George/Martha version.

Kabul looked primitive; there were few paved streets and we had been told that, until recently, packs of wild dogs roamed the night. The Soviet built theater was attractive but only the auditorium was heated, not the stage or backstage areas.

Our opening night audience included His Royal Highness Lemar-e-Ali Marshal Shah Wali, Their Royal Highnesses Lemar-e-Ali Sardar Mohammed Daud, Prime Minister of the Royal Afghan Government, and Lemar-e-Ali Sardar Mohammed Naim, Second Deputy Prime Minister and Minister of Foreign Affairs of the Royal Afghan Government. Their wives, whose names were a great deal shorter than their husbands but were princesses nonetheless, were resplendent in the latest Western fashions. The audience was filled with European and Soviet bloc ambassadors, but nary a soul who could be described as an ordinary citizen.

Of the few women we saw in public, most wore burkas (or chandors as they had been identified to us) with tightly embroidered latticework across the eye area. It was easy to understand why the men who were hired as our stagehands were distracted from their duties and stared at us unblinkingly. It had never before occurred to me that dancers clad in practice clothes could inspire prurient interest.

Gaping aside, our thoughts were on how to manage dancing in a theater that was so cold that we could see our breaths. Forty degree cold topped my list of the most difficult conditions under which I had ever performed. It was worse than dancing on clumps of crab grass in a backyard setting when I was nine years old. It was worse than dancing and falling four times on an oil-slicked stage in a small New England town. It was worse than dancing on Lisbon's thirty degree raked stage. In the cold it was impossible to warm up. Even beating our legs together in an entre chat quatre (jumping up and changing the legs from right leg front to left leg front and back again before landing) did not relieve the numbing sensation. Our ankles felt stiff and our breath was tight in our chests.

In an effort to ward off the cold, we women threw fat fear to the wind and thickened our legs with pink, nylon knit leg warmers under our pink Danskin tights. We wore wool cardigans under our costumes and stuffed the sleeves inside our bodices. The men, whose overdeveloped legs were more an asset than not and whose costumes were mostly long-sleeved, had an easier time adding and hiding the layers.

By the second performance, the stage had been warmed to a bearable level. In addition to backstage gas heaters, little wood burning stoves had been set near each wing, but noxious fumes felt like fire in our lungs and made us cough. My throat, already painful from a recent infection, was made worse by the looming *Dreams* premiere scheduled for the following evening. I would be too sick to dance.

My understudy wore my red, white, and blue tutu with the star spangled tiara. I am sure that stepping into the role was not her dream of glory, but I am also sure that she danced well and forgave me for not dancing. Meanwhile, I spent two days in my hotel bed with the covers over my head trying not to swallow. Even though saliva went down my throat with the ease of ground glass, I was comforted in knowing that if I had to miss a performance—the first and only one in my thirteen year professional career—this was the one to miss. In the end, the performance was not a disaster, permanently squashing any hopes we might have still held about the demise of this nightmare ballet.

The second performance of *Dreams* was in New Delhi, the first stop of a six-week tour in India, the last country we would visit before returning home. Mrs. Harkness would be in the audience. Surely she would see what the rest of us had known from the beginning; that the ballet had absolutely no artistic merit. Surely, that would be the end of Mrs. Harkness's interference with artistic policy. Surely, Bob would find another way to placate her. Of this I was confident.

As in every country we danced, the tasks of class and performance, the business of eating and washing tights, and the required socializing at Embassy parties kept us in a separate world. It was as though our reality was transported along with the trunks of costumes and crates of pointe shoes. It was jarringly incongruous when the cultural differences and, from time to time, political realities reminded us of our secondary roles as unofficial goodwill ambassadors.

All over Lisbon we saw scrawled graffiti, "Angola and Portugal" and "Angola will always be Portuguese." These were not positions held by the United States Government. Our two countries were further distanced by Portugal's lack of support for our recent stand in the Cuban Missile Crisis. However, people on the street and audience members alike greeted us warmly.

Of all the countries in all the foreign tours we visited, the American Consul in Jerusalem was the only diplomat whose sole interest in us was to inform us about the land in which we found ourselves. He invited us to his office where we sat and listened. This was not going to be a party. This would be a lecture with thoughts that chilled me.

During the Cold War, the greatest fear was World War III involving the Soviet Union. Conventional wisdom warned that it would start over the Berlin Wall. "Mark my words," we were told, "The Berlin Wall is not the problem. It is Jerusalem and the entire Middle East that we should fear." Three years later, in 1967, after the Six Day War, the West Bank would no longer be part of Jordan but be under Israeli control. And our stage manager would not have had to be nervous about his Jewish identity.

In Kabul, I learned that the Afghans, after having been refused military and economic financial aid from the United States, had turned to the Soviet Union. (I certainly could have guessed that our hotel had been built or, at least, designed by the Soviets since it looked like the hotels from the Soviet ABT tour. Public spaces and corridors were commodious, cold, empty, and void of charm.) More ominously, we were told that the West should feel no comfort upon hearing that some tribal factions had become disaffected with the Soviet presence. They were just as likely to resent us.

In Beirut, the "Paris of the East," we were the first guests at the new Hotel Phoenicia Intercontinental. On New Year's Eve, 1962, I drew the curtains open onto views of the Mediterranean Sea. In less than ten years, I would see pictures of the war-torn, seaside resort, including the ruined Phoenicia. I wondered about the people I saw living on the outskirts of the city in shacks of castoff materials, the most memorable of metal Coca Cola signs.

After performances in Amman, Jordan, and in the (then) Jordanian city of Ramallah, a State Department official wrote in his evaluation that the Jordanian press: "in the midst of taking broad editorial swipes at American policy in the Middle East ... felt constrained to say that ... (the Joffrey Ballet) was able to win the sympathy of the Arab audience. We have heard literally nothing but praise for the entire company as artists and people ... If the Department on occasion has doubted the wisdom of its presentations program, the Joffrey Ballet should reassure it that the program has a significant role and purpose."

In Amman, King Hussein asked to meet the company. Twenty-eight of us were driven to the palace gates, where all the cars were searched before we were allowed to proceed to the palace. We were ushered into a long reception hall. The room, with little sunlight, was austere. A table, long enough to accommodate perhaps thirty for dinner, ran down its center. Straight-back chairs were lined against the walls. We sat in a row along one of them. Two men dressed in ceremonial clothes with elegant, upswept, white turbans gave ten of us little cups and then with a skilled flourish poured a warm liquid from a long, spouted copper pot. Tasting like a combination of weak tea and weak coffee with a twist of perfume, we returned the empty cups with a shaking motion. Holding the cup steady indicated a request for a refill. The cups were then passed, unwashed, to the next ten of us.

Program (in Farsi and English) for command performance in Teheran, Iran, 1962. (Dancer: Francoise Martinet)

Finally we went into the King's private office. He wore a suit and tie. He was short, strongly built, handsome, charismatic, and only twenty-seven years old. I don't remember the niceties that were exchanged, but the king spoke perfect English and in the photographs taken by Albert Flouty, his official photographer, we seemed to be paying strict, polite attention. All the men in the company wore suits and ties and all the women wore stylish dresses. In one of the photographs, I had slipped off one of my three inch heeled shoes. The other women were standing in each of theirs. Bob looked very proud.

In Teheran, we were given an Iranian government handout. Under the heading, "Facts about Iran," there was a call for a National Crusade, a Holy War, designed to annihilate the Satan of illiteracy in all the villages and towns of Iran. Sounding like a worthy goal, I was taken aback when one of my friends told me that the Shah was not universally admired. Whispering, she told me about Savak, the secret police. I was not sure that I believed her.

After a week of performing, we were looking forward to our free day—a day during which we had planned a hiking trip to a nearby mountain village—when word that Shah Mohammed Reza Pahlavi wanted the company to perform for him. The very idea of a command performance conjured up royalty of centuries past. We agreed to give up our free day. All other thoughts were outweighed by excitement.

The sets and costumes from the closing night's performance were, at that moment, being loaded onto a cargo plane bound for the next city of our tour. They were intercepted at the last moment, a fitting prologue for a command performance in the Presence of Their Imperial Majesties, The Shahanshah and his Empress Farah Diba.

New programs were printed for the occasion, Their Imperial Majesties taking star billing above The Robert Joffrey Ballet. Although Xerox printing in early 1962 produced rather shabby results, the programs, after being enclosed in large bright green folders, looked worthy of any Excellency. The cover was embossed with the gold Pahlavi seal. This was not a seal of humility. A lion, a proxy for the Shah, I presumed, strode forward with a sword in his right paw. He stood in front of a sun and under an imperial crown. Performance preparations continued. The first three rows of audience seats were removed and were replaced with wonderfully woven, richly colored silk carpets and large, ornate armchairs. An audience of Iranian dignitaries and foreign diplomats was seated well in advance before the arrival of the royal couple.

We finished our class in a studio that was across an open courtyard from the theater. Staying behind to practice a few minutes longer, I found my way blocked by a soldier. He kept his machine gun pointed at me until one of his superiors came and let me pass. What threat could I possibly be, dressed in tights and leotard and carrying pointe shoes? I was a little annoyed but not nervous. I was more concerned about an endedans pirouette in Grahn's variation.

Pas de Deesses opened the program. We were gathered on stage, behind the curtain. There was a hush, an announcement in Farsi, and then the arrival of the Shah and his Queen. After they were seated, Françoise, dressed as Taglioni in a cloud of light blue silk, and I, in my cloud of pink, left the parted center stage curtain, each of us clutching a large bouquet of flowers. We tiptoed to the edge of the stage and down a few stairs until we were in front of Their Majesties. Françoise curtsied to the Shah and I to the Empress. They smiled. We smiled. We took a few steps backwards before turning to go back up onto the stage. We and Cerrito and Arthur St Leon took our opening pose and the curtain opened. When everything goes right in a performance, time seems to both stand still and rush by. I experienced this performance of *Pas de Deesses* in that quiet whirlwind.

The second ballet on the program was *Sea Shadows*, a lyrical, neo-classical adagio choreographed by Gerald Arpino for Lisa and Paul. The last ballet was *Fille Gardee* (*The Badly Guarded Daughter*) a comic ballet first choreographed in 1786. Fernand Nault's charming, miniaturized version had been reduced in length and cast size to suit our mid-size company. In this, as well as other ballets, I was in the corps de ballet. A no-star system meant that we who did leading roles did corps roles as well. Dancing in the corps never had the cachet of dancing a solo or principal role, but a compliment from Bob always kept my dancing light in spirit.

In January 1963 we left the Middle East for New Delhi. A newspaper, *The Times of India* described our "tumultuous welcome." The article continued, "Proceeds from the performances were earmarked for the Indian Defense Fund." (India and China were at war over their common border.) This information left me momentarily stunned. I had no idea that India and China were at war.

But again, I was soon consumed by performances and the preparation for what would become my favorite role.

In Amman, Jordan, with King Hussein, 1962. (Left to right) Francoise Martinet, Carina Rieger, Una Kai, Felix Smith, Marlene Rizzo, Suzanne Hammons, June Wilson, Helgi Tomasson, (behind) Jack Harpman, Lona Isakssen, (behind) Finis Jhung, Manet Seguin, Elisabeth Carroll, Vicente Nebreda, King Hussein of Jordan, Lawrence Rhodes, (behind) Nels Jorgensen, Lisa Bradley, Robert Joffrey, (behind) unknown, George Bardyguin, Brunilda Ruiz, Jeannot Cerrone, (kneeling) Paul Sutherland, the author, John Wilson, (behind) unknown, and Patricia Wilde. (photo credit: Albert Flouty)

Chapter 17

INDIA

Being in India in 1963 heightened both the senses and emotions. Over the six-week tour, there were many receptions held in our honor. During one of the first, our Indian host asked me, "And what is your first impression of India? The poverty?" I could not tell whether his expression was wry or condescending. Being an atomic scientist and an owner of textile mills, he was of a high caste in a country that officially had no castes. He was handsomely dressed in a Nehru jacket—the loose-fitting, small stand-up collar style that had traveled to the West for a wildly popular, short-lived life. He was very rich and light-skinned. His home, wife, and daughters were resplendent in color. The women wore silk saris with borders of silver and gold threads. Their jewelry adorned fingers, wrists, and necks; all of it a deep rich twenty-four karat gold. My eyes were drawn to the red dots on the women's foreheads and the tiny diamond each wore on one of their nostrils. Outsized blooms in bowls and vases graced every horizontal surface in their home.

I was determined to appear unflappable and sophisticated. "Well, yes, the poverty," I answered our host. "And also, color," I added with emphasis. He looked pleasantly surprised at my answer and began talking about architecture, Hindu religion, Indian classical music, and dance. Responding with interest and an occasional arched eyebrow, I thought I hid my absolute ignorance quite well.

We performed in New Delhi, Hyderabad, Ahmadabad, Madras, Bombay, and Calcutta. Each section of the country was distinct, not only in geography, language, and customs, but also in breed of cow. A lot of what I saw, heard, smelled, and tasted was steeped with the exotic or the bizarre. And although I was often charmed during our Indian tour, I was also horrified.

Having been brought up in the 1940s and 1950s in a middle-class, professional Boston suburb, my life was insulated. World War II, the Korean Conflict, and the feverish Cold War hardly impinged on my life. Starving children conjured up fewer images of war than a guilty reminder to finish the cooked carrots on my plate. In 1953 my parents were the last in the neighborhood to buy a television console. We watched Sid Caesar's *Your Show of Shows*, tedious lectures on the educational channel, and my sister's favorite show, *Howdy Doody*. Documentaries on poverty were nonexistent and I had never knowingly seen a homeless person.

Upon arriving in New Delhi we all were given "Welcome to India" kits and copies of a meticulously organized schedule that our hosts had prepared. The company's business and stage managers had preceded us by two days. Three trucks, five officials, and twelve "coolies" (as they were referred to in the schedule) met them. The dancers arrived by Aryana Charter and were greeted in a special section of Safdarjung Airport by seventeen people and fifty garlands of flowers. All of the young Indian women were impeccably polite and had names as intoxicatingly musical as their accents. Among them were Miss Rajika Palit, Miss Amrita Anand, and Miss Indra Jeswani. When they walked, they glided. They skillfully guided us to hotels, restaurants, and to the taxis that would transport us to and from the theater.

The following morning as we piled into waiting taxis, a jolt sent my heart racing. Little hands reached through the windows. Shrill voices were pleading, "Please, Mister, Miss, please, money, money." The children were six-years old or maybe ten. I opened my mouth to say something or maybe I had been gaping and I closed it. The driver, shouting angrily, turned the key in the ignition. Just before we sped away, one of the children thrust the stump of what had been his arm in the window. This last entreaty was silent. Not even his eyes spoke.

We were whisked away to the theater for the first of six performances in New Delhi. After the fifth performance and many more garlands, sets and costumes were transported to the new United States Embassy where we would participate in its official opening. The architect, Edward Durell Stone, designed both the Embassy and the Ambassador's residence in the international style of the day. The front of the embassy was flat with symmetrical cinder block-like bricks. Daylight entered from sliver-wide, recessed windows just under the overhang of the roof. To the left and in the near distance, was the residence, similarly built. The long, low roofs tilted backwards and were supported, in part, by a row of slender columns, creating an austere portico.

An outdoor stage had been built at the back of the ambassador's residence. Between the stage and rows of chairs was a swimming pool. Somewhat awkwardly, the musicians were placed off to one side. Surrounding the stage proscenium was a curtain as different from the beige practicality of civic auditoriums and from opulent velvet of opera houses that could be imagined. Brightly colored, hand woven, and hand embroidered, the cheerfulness of textile folk art gave our little stage the look and feel of a large puppet theater. In front of us, floating in the swimming pool, were candles. The tiny flames added to the toy-like effect as they flickered in the night-darkened water.

Ambassadors, their wives, and selected personnel from many of New Delhi's embassies were in the audience. While dancing in one of the ballets that evening, my eyes pierced through the blue-black nightfall to some of the guests in the first row. Among them were Ambassador Kenneth Galbraith with his wife Catherine, Prime Minister Jawaharlal Nehru, Indira Gandhi (a future Prime Minister), Mrs. Harkness, and, most significantly, Robert Joffrey. It was always to, and for, Bob Joffrey that I danced.

Two small tent-like rooms had been assigned as dressing rooms, one each for the girls and boys. These backstage homes were where we not only prepared for the performance but where, when the performance was over, we changed for the Ambassador's gala reception. After wiping our faces clean of stage make-up and arches, ankles, and legs of dirt that always seemed to filter through our tights, the women applied street make-up and rolled on expensive, sheer, nylon stockings. We took a final look at ourselves in our Saks Fifth Avenue party dresses, gifts from Mrs. Harkness. (Before leaving New York, Mrs. Harkness had instructed the women to pick out dresses and for the men to buy suits specifically for Embassy receptions. I do not remember what our dollar limit was, but I do recall her disappointment at how conservative most of us were with her money. I, however, did not disappoint her. Having chosen a dress fashioned from tapestry fabric that was heavy with muted orange and green velvet spirals—clearly the most beautiful dress ever made—I spent every dollar allowed.)

Leaving the dressing rooms, we dragged our packed theater cases. The men, trained to lift and throw ballerinas, handled their cases with ease. The women managed theirs well enough, especially considering that our cases, filled with extra pointe shoes and more bottles and jars, were heavier than the men's. Lithe and slender and, on party nights, dressed with glamour and very high-heeled shoes, our upper body strength was all the more impressive. On this evening, however, we needed to lug them only as far as the dressing room doors.

Upon arrival in each theater, it was our responsibility to locate our own theater cases and to return them at the evening's end, or, less often and more deliciously, after a whole week's worth of evenings. The cases—cardboard composition boxes three feet long by two feet wide and one foot deep—were stacked in open-sided, heavy, wooden boxes that had been wheeled somewhere out of the way in a backstage corner. Each box had two rows of cases, six cases high. Pulling two canvas straps tightly around our cases, it was possible to keep the bulging covers from popping so high that they couldn't be jammed into their respective slots. Although our names were on the cases, some of us further marked them for even easier identification. Giant white strips and X's stood out, thanks to white adhesive tape—a staple every dancer packs for foot care.

Walking to Ambassador Galbraith's residence where the reception was already in progress, we opened the door directly onto a large two-story reception room. I began jockeying around the smiling, slow-moving guests to the source of clinking glasses. Champagne in hand, I followed oval silver trays. Held aloft as they were moved around the room, they shimmered like great beckoning orbs. They were laden with lots of delectable things to eat. Post-performance, ravenous appetite appeased, I joined the rest of the guests. This was infinitely more fun than the bus tour's tea and cream cheese sandwich receptions to which we were accustomed. So, it was with surprise that I received a less than lackluster response from one Embassy official. "This is the third one of these parties I've attended today," he groaned.

Moving on, I took a close look around me. A narrow balcony, high enough to be not immediately noticeable from the door, skirted three sides of the room. "Isn't it wonderful to live here?" I exclaimed to Mrs. Galbraith with whom I had struck a conversation. "Well, no," look up there," she said, indicating the balcony. Closed doors placed in neat order around the balcony separated the family living and sleeping quarters from the reception area below. "There's no privacy," she complained. I had a fleeting image of her six foot, eight inch tall husband shuffling in slippers from one side to the other. Just at that moment in my peripheral vision, I saw the Ambassador bent over in conversation with Prime Minister Nehru. In his formal attire, it was impossible for me to continue imagining a late night kitchen raid for cornflakes or cookies. I concluded that there must be a private access for the family to get from the bedroom to the kitchen and back again, but Mrs. Galbraith was speaking with someone else and I never found out.

I made my way across the room to Bob Joffrey who was talking with the Prime Minister. With a nimble hop and skip, I was standing in front of them and holding out my hand. I smiled a broad stage smile. Bob responded with an introduction. Mr. Nehru seemed chilly. Maybe my eagerness was gauche, but I didn't care. I was going to be able to say that I had met Prime Minister Nehru.

Throughout our tour of India, taxi rides to the theater continued to rack me with images that would never leave. All kinds of transportation crowded the city streets. Cars, taxis, buses, human rickshaws, a grand piano balanced on the heads of five men, and the occasional cow all moved along together. Life expectancy for porters was thirty years. Life expectancy for cows must also have been short. Considered sacred, we were told that they were not slaughtered; although considering that they were kept alive by picking over already picked over garbage, the fate of becoming beef curry didn't seem much worse. One such miserable creature with a gaping hole in its side was able to keep pace, somehow, with the walking grand piano.

In each city, we dancers received glowing reviews. My friends and I were almost as happy for each other as we were for ourselves. All good reviews reflected well on the company, the company of which we were so proud. However, whenever my name appeared, it seemed to burst off the page, as it did in the review for the opening night's last ballet on the program, *Con Amore*. I was called a "delightful coquette" and a "sprightly flirt" and that I was "definitely the most outstanding of the half dozen featured players, giving the crowning touch to a performance of polished comedy and superb dancing." Although happy with good reviews, a dancer's happiness is contingent, in part, upon dancing new roles. And I wanted to dance the lead in a dramatic ballet.

Positioned in the middle of a program of short works, the dramatic or more avant garde piece is usually the one which gets the most attention and highest praise. After all, how can a mix of Amazons and a coquette, or even tutus and sylphs, compete with unrequited love, murder, or madness? It sometimes does, of course, but not usually.

Acting in a dramatic piece, not the actual execution of steps, is paramount. Ironically, the emotions released by acting can give an impetus to the technique making difficult steps easier and if, by chance, technique falters, they are more easily forgiven.

New York City Ballet premiered *Pastorale*, choreographed by Francisco Moncion in 1957. Reset for the Joffrey two years later, it had been in our repertoire for three years. I had waited a long time to be given a chance to do the lead. That opportunity was soon to be mine. When the company first learned the ballet, Bob had suggested to the choreographer that he cast the lead for another dancer and me, two of his older dancers. The choreographer chose a new member of the company as first cast, bumping me down from second cast to understudy. Now, in Madras, three weeks from the end of our tour, Bob said that I could do the ballet. Stealing time after classes and rehearsals to practice turns and lifts, I found Jerry Arpino, with whom I would be dancing, reassuring and inspiring.

The ballet opens with the Stranger, a blind man seated by a grove of stylized trees. He is handsome, mature, and, we soon see, romantic, in the manner of a nineteenth century poet. Next, a group of carefree friends playing Blind Man's Bluff (a game surely now renamed) enters and then runs away, leaving the Girl blindfolded and alone. She and the poetic Stranger meet. Light-hearted turns and twists evolve into more tender embraces. Then—suspecting that she is not with her boyfriend—the Girl tears off her blindfold. Finally and, at first, tentatively, their dance continues. The friends return and although torn between the Stranger and her friends, the Girl chooses her friends. The ballet ends with the Stranger alone on an empty stage. The story line in the ballet, as are many, is thin. The power is in the telling. And in dance the telling is told with music, choreography, and the hearts of the performers.

The day of my first performance had come. "Merde," my friends said. It was intermission between the first ballet and *Pastorale*. The stagehands were securing the small cluster of metal poles that would represent the trees. The cast of *Pastorale* began filtering onto the stage. Some of them practiced a step or two, some bent and stretched. I walked around the perimeter of the stage to get a better sense of the floor space and the reach of space above the proscenium and through the wings. The boundaries changed for me, not only by the sets but also by the character I would become. I could hear the musicians practicing in the orchestra pit, their sounds muffled through the curtain.

As I waited, I remembered another performance of *Pastorale*. It was the ballet in which I had fallen and had been dragged on my stomach, so intent were my fellow dancers on getting to their places on cue for the lead couple's entrance. Tonight, they would part for me.

The musicians stopped warming up. Jerry Arpino, who had been walking among the trees, put his hand on one of them and struck the opening pose. "Merde," he said to me and I knew that I would be safe in his hands. I took my place in the wings and became the Girl.

Towards the end of the ballet with the difficult technical passages completed, I was free to concentrate solely on acting. Jerry and I were center stage, facing each other. I was on one knee, the other leg stretched out behind me. Jerry was bent over me with one leg stretched behind him. Each of our legs formed a diagonal line, meeting at the top of a pyramid, our embrace. My skirt of lemon-yellow chiffon fell into soft ripples around me. My hair, held away from my eyes by a violet velvet ribbon, was long and trailed down my back. The preceding unrelenting choreography had left me gasping for breath. In a backbend, my windpipe was constricted. Jerry's arms were gently around me. "Surely, my poet will lift me up ahead of cue, if I wheeze much louder," I thought. I felt the side of his face against my chest. It was warm and wet with sweat. His make-up, a ruddy color, was imprinting on my pretty yellow bodice. Dampened, the faint odor of cleaning fluid from innumerable prior scrubbings became stronger. I did not choke. We stood on cue. Our embrace unlocked and we parted. The ballet had come to an end.

"That was very good," Bob Joffrey said to me after that first performance. Detecting a little surprise in his face did not lessen my joy for he had emphasized the word "very," and his eyes had sparkled. I was given additional performances both in India and in the upcoming Soviet Union and American tours. I had been upgraded from understudy to second cast.

At the close of the tour, we were told that we were scheduled for a second summer residency in Watch Hill, Rhode Island. The first one had preceded our Middle East/India tour. This one would precede a tour of the Soviet Union, the most exciting of the three tours on which I would ultimately go.

Chapter 18

WATCH HILL

The two summers we spent rehearsing in Watch Hill, Rhode Island were sponsored by Mrs. Harkness. Billed as "workshops," they were opportunities for Bob to hire choreographers to create new ballets for his company. The very definition of "workshop" meant that there were no performance deadlines, alleviating the almost certain stress of time constraints held over a choreographer's head. On the other hand, there was no guarantee that any of the ballets would be accepted into the repertoire, a situation that could not have been stress free. However, each choreographer had all the time and all the dancers that were needed. The summers were luxuriously long and working conditions were ideal.

Watch Hill was an exclusive, little resort town on the coast of Rhode Island. Mrs. Harkness's Holiday House, with its forty rooms, seventeen baths, and swimming pool, housed Bob, Jerry, guest teachers, and the choreographers. The choreographers arrived in overlapping shifts and we eyed each one with anticipation.

The dancers did not stay in the rock-perched mansion on the ocean side of town. Our accomodations were in a rambling wood apartment complex built for the vacationing middle class of Pawtucket and Providence. It was adjacent to an old firehouse that had been renovated into two large studios with mirrors, new wood floors, pianos (which were kept in tune), and high ceilings (thanks to Mrs. Harkness's having had the roof raised).

In New York, summer air was clammy from humidity and pollution. In Watch Hill, we pulled on practice clothes that were damp with sea air. Every morning in New York we rode the noisy, stifling hot subway to the Greenwich Village studios. In Watch Hill, we had a one-minute walking commute. Our feet, turned out and in sandals made slapping sounds as we went the twenty yards to the firehouse studios. Holding pointe shoes by the ribbons, we swung them lazily by our sides. In New York, sweat dried on our bodies and lunch was at a nearby drugstore chrome counter. In Watch Hill, we walked back to our apartments where we could shower and make our own lunches. In New York, rehearsal pay was at a subsistence level. In Watch Hill, we were paid union scale and we had weekends off. Outside the studio windows in New York was the din of traffic punctuated by shouts from the women's prison directly across the street. (Originally an 1876 Victorian Gothic courthouse, the building is now a library.) Friends, sometimes with small children, cried up to the women behind the small barred windows. In Watch Hill, the studios overlooked a small bay that shimmered with luminous wavy bits. Waking up in Watch Hill and eating breakfast to putting on practice clothes and walking to the studio was a seamless, organic-like transition to the day's first plié. For me, however, the distraction of sea air and sun made Watch Hill feel more like a summer dance camp than an authentic professional experience. I may have been the only dancer who was not happy those two summers.

I missed being in New York where I awoke early to allow for travel time. Over breakfast, I thought about the upcoming day and how much energy and passion each rehearsal would require. I walked two blocks to the subway, sat in the car with my large dance bag on my lap, and counted the stops as the train sped and clattered along. An ear-piercing screech or two or six, along with the vibration, assured total wakefulness upon reaching the West 14th Street stop. I walked briskly past pedestrians, shops, and restaurants to my 434 Sixth Avenue destination. In the dressing room, my friends and I chatted and once in the studio we continued chatting as we stretched out sore muscles from the previous day. This more jarring transition perfectly prepared my body and psyche for the day ahead.

My experience aside, the Watch Hill rehearsal workshops were fruitful months for the company. Among the ballets taken into the company were *Gamelan*, Bob's first new ballet in a number of years and Jerry's *Incubus* and *Sea Shadow*. *Gamelan* had a Japanese sensibility. Many of the women in the company—including myself—hoped to be given special parts, but Bob gave that honor to Lisa and yet another, second, young dancer with elastic limbs. The two female leads were held aloft, not in traditional showy-style lifts, but in such a way that they appeared to be moving on a level, airborne surface. Jerry's two ballets dwelled in completely opposite emotional realms. *Incubus* told of a young girl's agonizing nightmare demons and *Sea Shadow* was a romantic fantasy to a score that was reminiscent of the French Romantic era.

Brian Macdonald, a Canadian choreographer, had both of his ballets, *Time Out of Mind* and *Caprices*, accepted into the repertoire. They were at least as contrasting as Jerry's two ballets. *Time Out of Mind* was costumed in white tights and leotards and even by today's standards would be considered palpably sexual. Harkening back to some prehistoric mating ritual, we thought it was great fun to dance. It was certainly different from anything we had danced before. But it was in the much more conventional *Caprices* that I had a special part. With music by Rieti, *Caprices* was choreographed in sections, connected by its theme. A duet had been choreographed for Paul and myself. It was light-hearted and spirited, leaving me happily breathless.

Pas de deux and duets (both dances for two people) are choreographically different, distinguished by partnering or the lack of it. In a pas de deux the male dancer, often in a princely but subordinate role, presents his partner to the audience by enhancing her turns and balances by subtle manipulation and displaying her line and beauty in lifted aerial poses. In contrast, most jumps and turns in a duet are performed in unison, although a few partnered turns and lifts may be included. For the female dancer, more control is required in a pas de deux and more stamina in a duet.

Perspectives, another Watch Hill ballet, was the furthest from classical ballet technique that our young ballet company had ever undertaken. Anna Sokolow was a socially aware modern dancer and choreographer. Like the choreographer herself, there were no superfluous movements or unnecessary adornments in her work. Simple and powerful, the choreography seemed to warn of impending dangers in the atomic age. Anna Sokolow never told us what her ballet meant, but when I suggested my interpretation, she smiled and I like to think that she was pleased. I liked Anna Sokolow and was sorry that her ballet never toured with us.

The work of Alvin Ailey, an African-American dancer and choreographer, would become a popular ballet in our repertoire. Alvin reminded me of Bob Joffrey. They were short, muscular, young, and dynamic; they worked with single-minded intensity; and they both had companies that bore their names. Unlike Bob's company, the Ailey Company would principally perform Alvin's own work. We looked forward to rehearsing with him.

Which ballets would be rehearsed and with whom were thoughts never far from mind. Each evening at five o'clock the next day's rehearsal schedule (or call sheet) was promptly posted and we eagerly gathered around it. Thumb-tacked to a cork bulletin board just inside the firehouse building, the call sheet was composed of three pages, one page for each studio. The heading was always the same. "Company Class: 9:30-11:00" and under that, "Break: 11:00-11:15." The schedule, organized and written by hand took juggling skill to parcel out dancers, choreographers, and pianists between the two main studios in the firehouse and the third, smaller studio in Mrs. Harkness's Holiday House.

Occasionally, an assistant would interrupt a rehearsal in progress and, with controlled desperation, plead, "Excuse me, but there has been a mistake and choreographer X wants Joan or Bill," or some one of us. Only the more esteemed choreographers could ask to have another choreographer's rehearsal interrupted. They, of course, were rarely interrupted.

Quickly skimming over the schedule, our eyes alighted on our own names, which meant a solo or small group rehearsal, and the words, "full company." We planned our days accordingly. Solo parts received one-hundred percent effort. Corps parts also demanded full effort, but the bar was a lot lower. We took note of all the breaks, especially the lunch break.

We were particularly excited when Alvin's first rehearsal was posted. His ballet, *Feast of Ashes*, based on Federico García Lorca's novel, *House of Bernarda Alba*, had music by Carlos Surinach, some of which was composed specifically for the ballet. The basic story line revolves around a matriarch with five unmarried daughters and her efforts to get them married, beginning with the oldest. To this end, a young man is introduced. Skipping over the eldest and the next three in line, he falls in love with the youngest and she with him. Meetings, furtive and forbidden, only come to an end with the murder of the suitor by the men of the village.

The dark Goya-like plot reminded me of the lurking doom I felt in dank Spanish village churches. On the walls, paintings of anguished saints and sinners remained caught behind incense, dirt, and varnish. The lurking doom in *Feast of Ashes*, however, was unlocked by gesture and music, both fierce and impassioned.

Who would be the dancers called upon to bring this tale to life? Who would be the Young Man, the Youngest Daughter, and the Eldest Daughter? Although the Joffrey Ballet called itself a company of soloists and billing was in alphabetical order, there was a hierarchy nonetheless. The more senior dancers and I—at twenty-five years old and a company veteran of five years—expected to be considered for leading roles. The more recent company members would, more often than not, fill the secondary solo and corps roles. Customarily, choreographers became familiar with the company's dancers from having seen them in performance or in class. For further evaluation, choreographers often requested the participation of the entire company in their first few rehearsals. Last and never least, Bob made recommendations. Ultimately, however, a choreographer's choice was honored.

Within moments of Alvin Ailey's first rehearsal we knew which movements were meant for which parts. Beside the main characters, there were seven Men of the Village and two Loose Women. All of the men learned all the men's steps and all of the women learned all the women's steps. By carefully observing whom the choreographer was carefully watching we knew who was being considered for which parts. It looked as though one of the other senior dancers was slated for the youngest daughter role and that I was going to be the understudy. However, Lisa, the young dancer with the pliable body and delicate face, began to receive most of the choreographer's attention.

The following day's schedule was posted at its usual time and in its usual place. I stood in front of it. Scouring, checking, and rechecking it did not change it. Lisa had the leading role. She would be first cast. The dancer we thought would take that honor was now cast as one of the Loose Women along with being assigned as Lisa's understudy. My job was to understudy her lesser role. Eventually there would be another casting change. Lisa's understudy would be elevated to second cast and the Loose Woman role became exclusively mine, relieving the understudy of having to divide her attention between two roles. (It would be in this ballet that I was dropped in a lift. The red and orange ruffled costume with sewn-in padded breasts had undoubtedly protected me from a more serious fracture.) My heart sank. "At least," I thought, "I am not the Matriarch."

Being scheduled with one of the guest teachers for private or semi-private classes took the sting out of casting disappointments. Although having time for these classes meant, perhaps, not being used or wanted for a particular ballet, being chosen to attend the classes was itself an honor. They were always held in the small studio at the Holiday House.

Guest teachers Vera Volkova and Stanley Williams were connected to the Royal Danish Ballet. Madame Volkova, who had been a student of the acclaimed Russian teacher, Agrippina Vaganova, had herself become a legendary teacher. Stanley, a former principal dancer with the Danish Ballet, also had a superb reputation as a teacher, particularly for men. Madame Volkova used analogies to illustrate her teaching, successfully imparting the qualities she wanted emphasized. Thinking of reaching for a flower, for instance, automatically changes how the fingers are held or where the eyes are focused. Her teaching manner was fittingly gentle. Stanley Williams's much firmer demeanor was softened by his occasional baritone chuckle. Whereas Russian male dancers were famous for large, robust jumps, which seemed to draw up from the floor, Danish dancers were recognized by light buoyant jumps that seemed to have come from nowhere. Stanley would leave Watch Hill to become a principal teacher with Balanchine's New York City Ballet School.

The small Holiday House studio where we took these classes overlooked the open ocean. Waves crashing onto rocks below were even more of a distraction than the twinkling bay outside the firehouse.

Each day's class and rehearsal schedule determined which pointe shoes or ballet slippers would be needed. Pointe shoes required preparation time. Most of the women padded bumps, bunions, and blisters on their overworked feet. Using a razor blade, we cut open seams on the soles of our tights. Slipping our toes free from the pink, stretchy material, we applied tape, Band-Aids, bits of Dr. Scholl foam rubber, and dabs of lamb's wool. Protection completed, we stuck our toes back inside the feet of our tights. Then, just before actually putting on our pointe shoes, we wrapped the tips of our somewhat bulky toes in a layer of brown paper. Tearing off a scrap at a time, one A&P supermarket bag could last a few of us several days. Nothing was more efficient at absorbing sweat while at the same time not crumbling to bits.

Most ballets, but not all, required pointe shoes. Choreography began crossing over between ballet and modern dance in the early sixties. Not only did Bob engage Alvin Ailey and Anna Sokolow to work with us, but also ballet choreographers—Brian Macdonald and Gerald Arpino among them—began using freer and less classically based movements. These ballets, the word "ballets" used generically, were often danced in soft ballet slippers. I enjoyed dancing in the more modern ballets, but classical ballet remained my first love.

The one Watch Hill ballet that was uniformly disliked was the dreaded *Dreams of Glory*, music by Mrs. Harkness. Rechoreographed and renamed, *The Palace* was a pastiche of dances, inspired by 1920s vaudeville days. It now was a choreographic collaboration, which included work by Bob Joffrey and Gerald Arpino. Remaining intact was Mrs. Harkness's music, as annoying and cloying as ever. *The Palace* was the third and final choreographic effort to the Harkness *Dreams of Glory* score. It would be performed in Leningrad, Kharkov, Donetsk, Kiev, and Moscow. Jerry Arpino, choreographing most of the pieces, did a valiant and entertaining job. He included flappers, top hat strutters, bathing beauties, and something called "Miss Sunny and Her Cavaliers." This tribute to the 1920s was a big hit in the USSR. It would continue to be performed during the subsequent US tour.

Bob cast Paul and me in the "Pas de Deux Oriental," his choreographic contribution. The fluid lifts, turns, and balances, my see-thru harem pants, spangled bodice, and jeweled headband with its single white feather, and Paul's white tights and feather-topped purple turban did not exactly represent cultural authenticity, but it accurately represented the popular motif of all things à la Oriental in the 1920s and 1930s. It was the most technical role I danced.

After one *Palace* performance, I would earn a complement from Bob. And that performance was at the White House.

Chapter 19

WHITE HOUSE

The Robert Joffrey Ballet was the third ballet company to perform at the White House. Ballets USA was the first. Jerome Robbins—in popular culture probably best known as the choreographer of *West Side Story*—began his Ballets USA in 1957 to help inaugurate Gian Carlo Menotti's Festival of Two Worlds in Spoleto, Italy. The company disbanded in 1962 but not before dancing for the Kennedy-hosted State dinner in honor of the Shah of Iran.

In May 1962, American Ballet Theatre also performed at a State dinner, this time honoring the President and Madame Felix Houphouet-Boigny of The Ivory Coast.

Then on October1, 1963 the Joffrey Ballet danced at the White House. We performed in the East Room. JFK was still President. Most Americans were proud of the handsome, sophisticated first family. Jackie had bouffant hair, Caroline was nearly six years old, and John-John was three. Patrick, the Kennedy's infant son, had died three months previously and Jacqueline Kennedy, still grieving, left early that October evening to vacation with her sister, Lee Radzwill. They traveled to Greece where they were guests on Aristotle Onassis's yacht.

Rose Kennedy, the seventy-three old mother of the President, stood in for her daughter-in-law as hostess for the evening's festivities. Ethiopia's Emperor Haile Selassie along with Princess Ruth Desta, his adult granddaughter, were being honored by the President with a white tie, White House State Dinner. After dining on Boston sole diplomate, beef chevreuse, string beans, braised endive, and galante of chicken, the Emperor with his granddaughter and the President with his mother left the state dining room to join one hundred twenty-nine other guests in the East Room for a Joffrey Ballet performance. Among them were: Vice President Lyndon Johnson and his wife "Lady Bird;" Chief Justice Warren; United Nations Ambassador Adlai Stevenson; Undersecretary of State, Averell Harriman; Secretary of the Army Cyrus Vance; CBS Producer of the First Lady's Tour of The White House, Perry Wolff; president of ABC, Leonard Goldenson; and assorted

Listening to notes after dress rehearsal in the East Room at the White House. (Left to right) John Wilson, Vicente Nebreda, the author, and Helgi Tomasson, 1963. (photo credit: The Washington Post)

Congressmen, friends, and relatives. Stephen Smith, the husband of the President's sister, Jean, was also present and was overheard to say that he expected to begin campaigning soon for the President. It was a year away from the next presidential election. It was fifty-three days away from November 22—the day of the assassination that would shock the world.

A temporary stage had been erected at one end of the East Room. Plywood flooring covered with non-slick linoleum made a perfect dancing surface. Black cloth, stretched over wood frames made satisfactory wings and a backdrop. Visible beyond the top line of the backdrop were the tops of three window swags, plaster moldings, and pilasters. One of the East Room's large crystal chandeliers hung smack in the middle of the stage. It was fitting that turning one of the country's most important historic rooms into a theater was only a partial metamorphosis. The First Lady's love of the ballet and her interest in the arts would eventually result in the formation of the National Council on the Arts. The Kennedy Center would stand as a testament to her efforts. Leaving our Greenwich Village address on that early October morning, I remembered Bob Joffrey's earlier prediction that there would be an American national ballet company and that the Joffrey Ballet might be that company. Alas, that was not to be.

But taking my seat on our familiar charter bus on that day, dance bag and coffee in hand, I believed that our performance that evening would, indeed, be an auspicious event. Arriving in Washington we passed familiar postcard views of the city until, jumping to life, the White House came into view. We were let off at a side entrance. It was very quiet. We were very quiet. We were led upstairs to a family area where a door opened onto a carpeted room. Intent on finding a dressing room spot of my own, I chose a back corner in which to spread out and be by myself. Usually a routine ritual, this preparation for this performance was difficult. I was, after all, in the house of Presidents and the home of President Kennedy.

Immediately prior to the White House performance. Robert Joffrey greeting Princess Ruth Desta, granddaughter of Ethiopian Emperor Haile Selassie. Vice President Johnson is standing to the left. President John F. Kennedy is in the center. Chief Justice Earl Warren is seated to the right. Oct 1, 1963. (photo credit: Cecil Stoughton, White House/John F. Kennedy Presidential Library and Museum, Boston)

Bob gave us a warm-up class that was followed by a blocking rehearsal to help us adjust to the modest, though remarkable, stage. After a short break to put on costumes and pointe shoes, we had a dress rehearsal with the United States Air Force Orchestra, our musicians for the evening. The program opened with *Partita for Four*, the first of the many ballets that Jerry would ultimately choreograph. It was a charming ballet whose greater charm, perhaps, was its promise of maturing future work. The remainder of the one-hour program consisted of segments from *The Palace*. The composer, Rebecca Harkness, would be in the audience.

We gave little thought to the appropriateness of the program. Although some of the *Palace* segments were a trifle risqué, they were principally nostalgic roaring twenties Americana. Our repertoire for both the White House performance and the Soviet Union tour scheduled to begin in two weeks had been pre-approved in New York. It was assumed that both Mr. Wolf from the White House and Sergei Shashkine of the USSR booking agency had judged our programs as being neither too overtly sexual nor nationalistic. At the end of the dress rehearsal, as the musicians left for a dinner break, we heard that there was a problem.

Jackie Kennedy, unable to attend the performance, had watched the rehearsal with her children and her secretary, Nancy Tuckerman. Although we understood that Mrs. Kennedy was reluctant to interfere, she insisted that the program be modified. The Emperor had become religious, she said, and she feared that some of the dances would offend him.

Our White House performance followed Ballets USA in controversy. (Evidently, no trace of salaciousness had been detected in American Ballet Theatre's offering of *Billy the Kid*.) One of Jerome Robbins ballets, *Opus Jazz*, was described by the Washington Evening Star staff reporter Betty Beale: "Hip swinging, torso-tossing, Robbins choreography at times seemed rather strong stuff to be serving up to visiting royalty." And what would she say about us?

After discussions with Mrs. Kennedy, Bob, Jerry, and Mrs. Harkness, compromises were reached. The (bathing) "Beauties of the Twenties" was entirely omitted and the "Charleston" was stripped of suggestive steps and gestures. Last minute telephone calls to area stores assured more modest costumes. Flesh-colored leotards were added to some of the women's costumes and black pants replaced the men's black tights. Paul's and my costumes were brought to Mrs. Kennedy where they passed inspection, as did, the amended ballet. The show would go on.

Betty Beale in her reporting of our performance, however, wondered about the "thoughts going on in the mind of the Emperor of Ethiopia as the philosophical face surveyed the 'Roaring Twenties' antics on the stage." She went on to describe,

"Girls in loose, above-the-knee, beaded dresses ... sashayed onto the stage ... and a chorus of vamp types of four decades ago—So one can't help wondering what His Imperial Majesty thought of it."

Paul and I assumed that our pas de deux was above reproach and that if Mrs. Kennedy had seen it, she would have approved. Unfortunately, she had arrived late to rehearsal and Paul and I had just finished. Even though there was no danger of her censoring our grandiose pas de deux, Bob asked us if we would repeat it. "This may be your only chance to dance for the First Lady," he said. Since it was characteristic for Bob to command, not request, I was grateful to him for the opportunity to refuse. It had taken all my energy to tamp down the nervousness that had welled up into my body and to do a good rehearsal. And now that it was over, my whole being was in a deep sigh of relief. Although I was prepared to repeat the effort once again later for the performance, I was unsure about my being successful on a third try. I was grateful to Bob for giving us the choice and I never regretted my decision not to dance for Jackie Kennedy.

Stage fright is common among many performers. The source, frequency, and severity are as varied as the legions of dancers, musicians, actors, orators, mimes, tumblers, and trapeze artists that have ever graced a stage or faced an audience. Fortunate are those who have found their own personal exorcism for setting their demons at bay. Failure to do so risks incapacitation.

My own demon visited me when I was fourteen years old while dancing on my junior high school stage. My legs became wobbly. My breath seemed caught in my throat. My mind went blank and I could not unglue my eyes from their unblinking, unseeing stare. Somehow I got through the performance although it certainly was not my best effort. Dancing behind me, were four younger schoolmates for whom I had choreographed a few steps while I, of course, was in front as the soloist. One of the dancers who was only twelve-years old was an exceptional talent and competition I had not expected. I was numb from comparing myself to her. It was a small thing in my life but it had a big impact. The young dancer was Eleanor D'Antuono who would eventually become a principal dancer with American Ballet Theatre and a good friend. She taught me, by example, to focus on the task at hand, a lesson made difficult by the fear of again being overwhelmed by fear. Over the years, I learned to subdue this lurking nightmare by saying to myself, "What is this one ballet to the entire program? What is this program to all of the programs on the tour? What is the tour to my career, my career to my life, my life to the lives of all beings on the planet, the planet to the universe, and the universe to the galaxies?" By repeating this prayerful litany before each performance, I was able to hold stage fright at bay. I dared not doubt its power.

The East Room at the White House. The author and Paul Sutherland in The Palace, *"Pas de Deux Orientale" choreographed by Robert Joffrey. Lisa Bradley is in the wings. Oct 1, 1963. (photo credit: Cecil Stoughton, White House/John F. Kennedy Presidential Library and Museum, Boston)*

Waiting in the wings to dance before our august White House audience, stage fright threatened to pitch me over the edge. I repeated my magic words over and over, each time with more fervor than the last. Finally, Paul and I walked on stage and took our beginning poses. My body was now under my control. I waited to begin. I set my gaze well beyond the center spot of the front row where John Kennedy was sitting. For a fleeting second, we shared the same anticipation. He also was waiting for the pas de deux to begin.

We began alone, center stage. Paul was in a lunge to my side and facing me. I was facing the audience on pointe with feet crossed and held tightly together in fifth position. My arms were in a circle above my head. Turning my head and giving my partner an imperious glace, I placed my right hand into his outstretched hand. Again facing the audience, I drew my left foot, still tautly pointed, up the front of my right leg to just below the knee before continuing up to the inside of the leg for several more inches before forcefully, but smoothly, pulling my knee as high as it could reach. In one flowing movement I continued unfolding the leg to a fully stretched position as close to my ear as my extension would allow (the step is appropriately named "développé"). Now, still on the toes of my right foot, my left leg held high to the side and my hand still pressed down on Paul's, I felt the muscles of both legs from my toes through my ankles, knees, thighs, and buttocks tighten. I locked my arms in their shoulder sockets and flattened my stomach further. I pulled my right shoulder and hip open against the opposing pull of the extended left leg. A final extra stretch to my already pointed left foot gave a beautifully arched finish, I hoped, to the leg in the air and to the pose that I would soon be holding, unaided by my partner. To balance on pointe in a highly extended position for six seconds is excellent; three seconds is good; and just not falling can be good enough. My balance was somewhere between three seconds and good enough. The pas de deux continued. Balances, turns, and lifts progressed easily and unerringly. And then it was over.

We had been told not to immediately change back into street clothes. We were a motley group. The women from the "Whiz Bangs" (flappers) segment wore bright red costumes with matching bow lips painted into a pout. Their identical coal black wigs sported the popular bobbed hairstyle of the era. Thick, large, black, spit curls were plastered against their cheeks. The men were conservatively dressed in light blue velvet jackets and pink bow ties. Paul and I were in our pink and purple costumes, glittering in fake Orientale regality.

Haile Selassie, the President, and Rose Kennedy were waiting for us in a receiving line. One at a time we met and shook hands with Emperor Selassie, whose regal credentials were unmistakably authentic. Over a plain white dress shirt and black tie, he wore a khaki jacket. Along with a thick gold braid that looped over his right shoulder, gold epaulets, and a black and gold belt, the left side of his chest was resplendent with three large, gold medallions and a row of ribbons. Sixteen ribbons, each with a small dangling medal, filed across his chest from armpit to the center gold button on his jacket.

Standing beside his guest, the President, in a formal white tie tux and a white carnation boutonniere, smiled broadly at each of us as he said, "Thank you." Rose Kennedy was elegant in aqua blue, three strands of pearls, and long white gloves. I was excited and overwhelmed at meeting these guests of honor.

Immediately after the White House performance. Greeting the dancers are Ethiopian Emperor Haile Selassie, President John F. Kennedy, and Rose Kennedy. Robert Joffrey is standing in back and to the left of Haile Selassie. Waiting to meet the honored guests (left to right) Paul Sutherland (in the turban), the author, James Howell, Brunilda Ruiz, Vicente Nebreda, Lawrence Rhodes, and Carina Rieger. Gerald Arpino is two rows behind Paul Sutherland. Senator Robert Byrd is in the lower left hand corner. Oct 1, 1963. (photo credit: Cecil Stoughton, White House/John F. Kennedy Presidential Library and Museum, Boston)

Before I left the room, I took a quick look around. A string quartet was playing in one corner. All the guests were dressed in timeless formal attire. Their grooming reflected a conservative sixties taste. The men had slightly full, short haircuts.

Carefully teased hair (that 1960s method of matting hair for extra volume) added an inch or two of salon-stiffened height to the women. Several men, dressed in black suits, looked as though they might have been from the secret service. An official White House photographer was taking pictures and a young Senator Robert Byrd from Virginia was close by. I looked back at Bob standing near the Emperor. Still only in his thirties, he looked even younger. How proud he looked!

I picked up a program that had been left on a table. Folded, it was three and a half inches by five inches and printed on heavy stock paper. On the cover was a small seal of the United States embossed in gold. Just below in black lettering was The Robert Joffrey Ballet. Below that, in smaller lettering, it said, "presented by The Rebekah Harkness Foundation" and at the bottom, "In Honor of His Imperial Majesty, The Emperor of Ethiopia, Tuesday, October 1st, 1963. The White House." I opened the program to the list of ballets, composers, choreographers, and dancers. I was taken aback and, then, heartsick. Where was the "Pas de Deux Orientale?" Where was Paul's and my name? They were not there.

The next morning, in our New York studio, I asked Bob, "Why?" "I didn't think that you would be ready," he said simply.

As it happened, I was ready and Bob said that I had danced well. I turned my attention toward the Soviet tour.

Chapter 20

AGAIN, OFF TO THE SOVIET UNION

We were off! It was October 10, 1963. We were scheduled to arrive in Leningrad late the next day. This would give us three days to prepare for our all-important opening night at the legendary Kirov Theater.

None of ABT performances had been booked into this magnificent theater, an exquisite, nineteenth century opera house with its plush blue and gold interior. Before the revolution, the theater and its resident opera and ballet companies were known as the Mariinsky. The Mariinsky, a name synonymous with Russian ballet stars and premieres of *Swan Lake* and *Sleeping Beauty*! Although we were scheduled to dance at the Mariinsky only on opening night, none of us could have been happier. To dance on the great stage even once was a rare privilege and the prospect of dancing solo roles increased both excitement and apprehension.

We were few enough in number to be booked not on a chartered plane but on a regularly scheduled airline. I braced myself for another twelve-hour overnight flight. Jet plane travel was still expensive so, again, I made the trans-Atlantic crossing to the loud hum of a propeller plane. Joffrey dancers were better behaved than the American Ballet Theatre dancers. Although our average ages were probably the same, we were less experienced and less independent than our Ballet Theatre counterparts. We drank less, smoked less, and stayed quietly in our seats longer. As before, the US and USSR carriers were not allowed to land in each other's countries. Whereas with ABT we flew directly to Paris for a connecting Aeroflot flight to Leningrad, the Joffrey company first flew into London's Heathrow Airport where we had an hour and a half layover before boarding for Paris. As before, a waiting Russian charter jet would whisk us off to Leningrad.

Arriving at Heathrow, the company lumbered sleepily off the plane. My feet were swollen, a common consequence of long propeller flights. It was impossible to shove my feet into shoes, but by breaking down the backs of my expensive leather heels and walking on the balls of my feet I managed to totter down the stairs off the plane. Shuffling through the airport to the "loo," I hoisted my legs, one heavy limb at a time, over a sink. I ran cold water over my pudgy feet and watched them slowly deflate to their normal size. I glanced once or twice at a few belongings I had placed on an adjacent sink. A few minutes before, Paul had given me our writing case that held a long letter in progress, two packets of lightweight airline stationery, matching envelopes pre-stamped "par avion," and both of our passports.

With my feet back inside my shoes, I rejoined my friends in aimless pacing until we were, at long last, back in the air and on our way. After a quick nap I heard, "Madames, Monsieurs." Our Air France hostess was welcoming us to Paris. We stood in the aisle, waiting to disembark. A flight of metal stairs was wheeled to the plane's front exit. "Get the passports," Paul said to me. My stomach turned. "Oh, no," I cried.

"Don't worry," Jeannot Cerrone, our general manager, said to me in English and "Mademoiselle," he continued in French once we stepped inside the Paris Orly Airport. Jeannot, who spoke several languages, had years of guiding ballet companies through airports and red tape. He was a well-liked, big-boned, attractive man whose paternalistic authority could fix all things. I remained nervous, however, waiting for him to return with a solution. The rest of the company had gathered in a waiting area preparing to board the Aeroflot jet. Before long, Jeannot returned with excellent news. The case with the passports had been found and would be sent to us within the hour. My sigh of relief was brief. The Russians could not, would not, and did not wait. "Don't worry," Jeannot said again. He gave us French francs, an address of a friend who owned a small hotel in Paris, and Air France tickets bound for Moscow the next morning. Although our final destination was Leningrad, Jeannot reassured us. "Close enough," he told us as he outlined the plan. A Russian interpreter would meet us in Moscow and take us to the American Embassy where we would be picked up and put on an overnight train later that evening. On the morning of October 13, after three days of not dancing, we would arrive in Leningrad and rejoin the company.

Ballet dancers generally do not take more than one day off a week and still, on the following day, they complain of stiffness and being out of shape. Paul and I would not only be off for three days, but we would have one fewer rehearsal days than the rest of the company. By not participating in the full rehearsal schedule on the famous and raked Mariinsky stage, I was certain that I would dance badly. My life would be over. As the chain of events ultimately unfolded the situation would become worse, resulting in my engaging in yet one additional long day of weeping and sobbing.

We said goodbye to Bob and waved to the rest of the company as they left. Within the hour, as had been promised, our passports were returned to us. We took a taxi to the center of Paris. Anxiety overcame any interest we would normally have had at seeing L'Arc de Triumphe and La Place de la Concorde. Our driver pointed to the fare. We counted out our francs and walked into a very small hotel lobby. Feeling like a school child with a note from home that always, back then, made everything alright, I gave Jeannot's letter to the man behind the desk. My meager French was more than sufficient to understand his response. He had no room for us. Did my fresh outburst of tears help? He made several phone calls and after a ten minute walk we were signing a registry at a different small hotel. We ate an excellent dinner in the hotel's restaurant and climbed three flights to our room for a fitful night's sleep.

The following day we were at Orly Airport at noon for a one-thirty departure, way too early back in the days of moderately busy passenger travel and no time-consuming security issues. Although delays and cancellations were rare, flights were susceptible to weather conditions. During the early morning hours of October 13, Paris was overhung with fog. All flights were backed up for hours. We took seats in one of the rows of long benches and waited along with scores of other passengers. The airport had sky-high ceilings and walls lined with ticket counters from every imaginable airline. A giant wall-board posted flight numbers, destinations, and departure times. "Click, click, click," the clatter of mechanically turned letters and numbers could be heard over the din.

Preceding the updated information, were loudspeaker announcements. "Ding, dong, ding," they began with a sweetly toned bell and were followed by an equally sweet voice. "Madames, Monsieurs," it said as it prepared passengers for imminent boarding. Spoken first in French and then in English with a French accent, the words were hypnotic. By two o'clock they had become monotonous. We had not eaten since the previous evening and I was feeling light-headed. I was five feet, six inches tall, weighed one-hundred and ten pounds, and tended to have low blood sugar. However, we dared not leave for the airport restaurant for fear of missing our plane. In 1963, and particularly in France, it was impossible to grab a fast food snack. Nor were we anywhere convenient to the duty-free stores where, hours before, I had spotted Belgian chocolates. Digging into the bottom of my dance bag I found six chocolate Hershey kisses, and placing them one at a time on my tongue, I made a game of how slowly I could dissolve them. The day droned along.

At a quarter to four we saw the words, "Air France" and "Moskva," on the wall. The flight and gate numbers rotated and clicked into place, indicating that departure was imminent. "Oh, no," I said. We had missed hearing the "Madames, Monsieur" announcement. How was that possible? "Does Moskva sound so very different than Moscow?" I asked Paul. We certainly had not been dozing and neither had we been distracted by talking to one another. From the hours of sitting and watching, we knew that the majority of our fellow passengers had already dashed to the gate. "Oh, no," I said again.

We tore down a flight of stairs into a small waiting room where just outside the door and on the tarmac was an empty bus. Disconcertingly, we were the only passengers. The three people who soon arrived provided no comfort. They were a middle-aged Italian woman and two small children. The woman was whimpering and the children looked frightened. The woman struggled as she dragged two wheel-less suitcases behind her. (No suitcases had wheels in 1963.) They proved to be heavy even for Paul who could hoist even his slightly hefty female partners.

"I'll carry them," he gallantly offered after someone instructed us to take seats on the waiting bus. Although we expected to be driven to the runway at any moment, we were concerned. We five were the only passengers and no others joined us. The minutes were passing. "Don't worry," we were assured by passing Air France personnel, "You are in the right place."

The silver outline of an airplane caught my eye. It was taxiing down a runway. "That's our plane," I yelled. Never before had I so desperately wanted to be wrong. I wasn't. "Stop the plane!" Paul shouted. The plane was not going to be stopped. Paul grabbed the Italian woman's two suitcases and I carried the small bag we had used for our Parisian overnight. "Follow me," Paul said as he bounded up the stairs and through Do Not Enter doors. The Italian woman was near hysteria. She was delivering the two children to their parents at the Italian embassy in Moscow. The children, six years old and the other about two years younger, were tugging at her coat. They were crying. My eyes, already burning from crying and lack of sleep, teared up. "Oh no," I repeated. Missing the plane meant our having yet another day without class and rehearsal.

The situation worsened. It was bad enough not to reach Leningrad until the day of our opening night. But we were told that the earliest plane to Moscow would not be until the following day, which meant that we would reach Leningrad on the day after the Joffrey opening. "Unacceptable!" Paul began shouting again. "Unacceptable!" I echoed. Finally, we all were given alternative bookings to Prague where we could connect with a Czechoslovakian flight to Moscow the next morning. No one in Paris could guarantee our getting seats for that leg of the journey, but it was close enough. I found myself repeating Jeannot's phrase of the day before. Even considering that our final destination would still be an overnight train-ride away, just getting inside the Iron Curtain really did seem close enough. We demanded that Air France make three calls, one each to the American Embassies in Prague and Moscow and a third to the Joffrey Ballet in Leningrad.

Communication before faxes, e-mails, and satellite phones was not easy but I had faith in Air France.

Having to wait two hours before our flight to Prague, we were offered free meals at a restaurant. Paul with the two suitcases, the Italian woman with the two children, and I gratefully accepted. We quickly ordered and then hungrily ate the bread set before us. Soon after the meals were served, an Air France representative came breathlessly into the restaurant. The plane was boarding. We had to follow her immediately. We did. The children cried. I controlled myself. We boarded.

At ten o'clock that night we arrived at the Prague airport, a small building with one ticket desk. The only employee on duty, by the greatest good luck, spoke English. Although our Italian companions had no problem traveling into the city for accommodations, we, as American citizens in a Soviet Bloc country without visas, were forbidden to leave the airport. Not only had Air France not notified the American Embassy of our arrival but because of the lateness of the hour there was no one to call for permission. I looked around. There was no food, the wood benches looked hard, and the air was chilly.

The timing of the Joffrey Ballet's visit was politically sensitive. It was not as strained as it was in 1960 over the U2 spy plane incident when we were with ABT, but all of the Cold War years were years of intense suspicion and mistrust. Nuclear warheads were poised in the direction of each other's major cities and many believed that war was inevitable. Soon after the start of our Joffrey tour, Charles Barghoorn, a Yale political science scholar who served in the press section of the American Embassy in Moscow, was arrested on espionage charges. (Under pressure from President Kennedy he was soon released.) But even without a politically charged incident, Americans without visas were unlikely to receive special treatment and that was just what we were asking for. And special treatment was, eventually, what we got. Paul and I were driven, along with our Italian companions, to a hotel in Prague's city center. We were told not to leave the hotel and to eat only at the hotel dining room, instructions we had no intention of breaking. We never did talk to anyone at the American embassy. Our passports listed our occupations as ballet dancers. Did our insistence that we were en route to Leningrad to perform at the Mariinsky Theater impress the fellow behind the desk? Did he feel sorry for us?

I never knew, but I hoped he realized how grateful we were. We spent the night in a comfortable hotel and enjoyed a hearty dinner of cabbage and meat. The restaurant was brightly lit and the patrons fit comfortably in their chairs as they laughed and ate. The night before in Paris the food had been delicately seasoned and the diners—after having selected just the right wine—spoke in hushed voices.

In Prague, the conversation was lively and loud and it made me feel happy. I felt reassured. Everything was going to be all right after all. I ordered a beer.

The next morning, the five of us met in the lobby. Paul again picked up the suitcases and we left for the short walk to the airport bus. Even though we turned right instead of left, extending our walk by twenty minutes, the remainder of our passage to Moscow was uneventful.

Upon landing, we bid goodbye to our Italian companions and watched the children and their joyous parents greet each other with impassioned hugs and noisy kisses.

The phone call to the American Embassy had gone through; a Russian interpreter met us. Marina pulled us quickly through checkpoint gates and by snappy looking officials. "You are separate from your group!" Marina translated as one of them cried out after us. Then she grumbled, "Stupid!" as she pushed us along. Once outside, she offered to drive us to the American Embassy where she said she would pick us up at nine o'clock and take us to the over night Moscow/Leningrad train. Then, as an after thought, she suggested, "Instead of my driving you to the embassy, you may prefer to walk. It is only a twenty minute walk and you need only walk in a straight line." After three days of stale airport and airplane air, the cool afternoon felt both tranquil and bracing.

Soon after striking out on our own, a little thrill of adventure struck my heart. Here we were, in Moscow, the setting of so many American espionage books and movies. Like being read to from a fairy tale as a child, the thrill was exciting, not frightening. This is going to be fun, I thought.

We knew that the American Embassy was on Tchaikovsky Street. We did not have the address written in the Russian alphabet. We did not know how to say American Embassy or Tchaikovsky Street in Russian. We did not have an English/Russian dictionary. Neither did we have rubles, kopecks, nor, obviously, good sense. We began and found ourselves walking through a labyrinth of apartment buildings under construction. Cement mixers and scaffoldings and bulldozers and other hard hat related equipment surrounded completed ten story buildings and nearly finished buildings. With the workmen gone for the day, the buildings looked as though they had just grown on their own out of the acres of treeless, rutted ground. We dared not circumvent the area. We had been told to walk in a straight line and that was exactly what we were going to do.

The twenty-minute walk reached the thirty-minute mark. I swallowed my rising fear. Eventually we were in the midst of wide streets, people, cars, and, because it now was dusk, lit streetlights. We spoke to our first Muscovite. "Americansky Embassy?" we asked hopefully. "Tchaikovsky Street?" we continued while pointing towards the upcoming intersection. No response. "Americansky Embassy?" we repeated with accompanying pantomime. Shrinking from us, men and women closed their coats tighter around their bodies and hurried on. Did they not understand us? Did they think that we were crazed foreign spies? A few people did understand and answered but, of course, we could not understand them. We followed, however, in the direction in which they pointed, hoped for the best, and then began all over again, "Americansky Embassy?" At long last, after another plea of "Tchaikovsky Street," we heard one of the few Russian words we knew. "Da!" We had found Tchaikovsky Street! We were no longer lost. We turned left along our precious Tchaikovsky Street. We found the American Embassy.

We rang the bell and a junior officer answered. "I've been waiting for you," he said. It had taken us three hours to reach him. He took us to a lounge area and gave us sandwiches. We chatted comfortably together.

At nine o'clock we left to meet our translator, Marina. The gate to the compound opened. Marina with a car and driver were waiting in the street. The gate to the compound closed behind us.

We sped to the train station. Now we truly were getting closer to Leningrad and the Kirov (Mariinsky) Theater. We were escorted onto the Red Arrow Express and to our sleeping compartment. "Do you have any money?" Marina asked as she gave us kopecks for tea. Before she left, she spoke to a woman dressed in a white apron and small white cap. This was the woman who would make tea for the passengers in our car. Her uniform looked like the one I was forced to wear in the late 1940s for junior high school in home economics (cooking and cleaning) classes. Our Russian lady's uniform, as well as mine in junior high, was meant to convey efficiency. In addition and rather unsettling, our tea lady's uniform sent a twin message of grim authority. There would be no nonsense anywhere near her cubicle at the far end of the car.

After carefully counting kopecks into her hand, she poured two glasses of hot dark tea. Russian tea making had an aura of alchemy. Hot water was poured from a brass samovar, a tall, bulbous container. In the center core of the samovar was a tube filled with hot coals that kept the water hot for many hours. Glasses (never cups) of tea were served in tea holders called "podstakanniki" (literally, under the glass). The stainless steel holders and handles were decorated with curved, rococo flourishes of tea vines, berries, and leaves. Space travel was another popular motif. My hand circled around a handle of tiny sputniks and a globe, crowned by the Kremlin's Spassky spire and its five-pointed star.

I dropped four sugar cubes into my tea and went into our sleeping compartment. There were four bunks, two on each side, one on top of the other.

Paul and I sat on one of the lower bunks and held our tea. I took my spoon and smashed the sugar. I remembered these heat resistant, iron cubes from the ABT tour. Russians held the cubes behind their teeth as they drank, undoubtedly the cause of the many stainless steel smiles we saw.

The coal powered train pulled out of the station. It was soon too dark to make out any villages or landscapes we might have passed. A little table covered with a paisley cloth sat against the window between the two sets of bunks. A tiny lamp with a burgundy lampshade and yellow fringe gave the compartment a charming, if seedy, 1920s appearance. None of the bunks had privacy curtains.

Sharing the compartment were two hefty, older men who seemed to be strangers to one another. Wordlessly, we each climbed into our bunks. Unpinning my hair and braiding it into one long braid down my back was the only part of my bedtime ritual I performed that night. Except for shoes, each of us was fully clothed. I burrowed into the blanket and wondered how well I would dance at the Mariinsky performance that would be underway in less than twenty-four hours.

I was too tense to be tired. "Nothing else can go wrong," I whispered up towards Paul's bunk. Then, one of our compartment mates began to snore. The bear-like sound fit his burly frame and it was continuous except for the few times it changed over to a saliva-filled spluttering. I lay awake. At five o'clock in the morning I gave up and got up. I wrapped my braid into a bun and slipped into my shoes. With the last of the kopecks, I went to the end of the car and the tea lady. Two hours later, at seven o'clock, we arrived in Leningrad.

Over the past four days, we had passed through five airports in five countries as well as the railway stations of Moscow and Leningrad. Except for the Czechoslovakian airport, they were all monumentally large and whirlwinds of confusion. We looked for Jeannot. "Where is he?" I asked into the air. He was not there and even though I knew that Marina was back in Moscow, I squinted my eyes and peered through the crowds in the hope of seeing her. "Come," I said to Paul, "We'll stand in the ticket line. Someone there will speak English." No one did but an official appeared from a back office and listened to us. "Americansky Ballet? Joffrey? Mariinsky? Hotel?" I accompanied each word with pantomime and panic. He nodded and led us across the street to a hotel where the receptionist spoke English. Although suspicious, she made a couple of phone calls. Since there were only two hotels for foreigners in the city it did not take long for her to announce, "The Astoria." The sympathetic man from the station led us back outside to the taxi stand where there was a substantial queue. He pushed us to the front. It was a pouring, cold, mid-October rain. He shoved us inside the first taxi that drove up over the loud objections of the waiting, wet Russians. He answered gruffly.

"Americansky Ballet," he said. "So much for public relations," I thought. Nevertheless, I sank gratefully into the seat.

We arrived at the Astoria just in time to join the company in the hotel dining room for breakfast. "You won't believe the problems we've had," someone began. The company, instead of being given the stage on which to rehearse as had been promised, was only given access to one of the theater's practice studios. I was not the least bit sympathetic. "Oh," our friend interrupted herself, "Where have you been all this time?" "Well," I began answering and then I hesitated. It was time to leave for the theater. My attention turned to the day's work and the eight o'clock curtain for the performance of a lifetime.

Chapter 21

CHEERS

There were four ballets on the program for our October 15, 1963 opening night. The first, *Feast of Ashes*, was renamed *House of Sorrows* by Soviet censors, thereby eliminating all religious symbolism that the title might have been suggested. (Ash Wednesday signifies the start of Lent.) The overtly sexual *Time Out of Mind* was also renamed. Presumably, the prehistory title of *Dawn of Humanity* gave the ballet respectability. Bob's poetic *Gamelan* was sandwiched between the two. *The Palace*, our upbeat, full cast ballet, was the evening's finale, as it would be on many of the tour's programs.

The sets and costumes for three of these ballets, along with all the piano rehearsal scores and pointe shoes, had been held up in Germany. Those potentially permanent losses caused more immediate concern then the whereabouts of Paul and me. Most leading roles had understudies and those ballets that didn't could be accommodated by either changing the choreography or, as in *The Palace*, eliminating the segment entirely. The possibility of our being permanently lost, I assume, never crossed anyone's mind.

The rehearsal pianists rose to the challenge by calling on their memories and improvisational skills, which they did admirably. Replacing sets and costumes would have been more difficult, necessitating the use of, hopefully, suitable costumes from either other ballets in our repertoire or borrowed ones from one of the Russian companies. In either case, piecing together appropriate sets and costumes would have required ingenuity.

The loss of pointe shoes would have been, by far, the most serious problem and the one that would have caused the greatest fear and consternation among the dancers. Although each of us carried several pairs in our theater cases, they would not last long. Using Russian made shoes was not a viable option. Although all shoes are made basically the same and may look the same, they can be as varied as an individual dancer's foot. It takes trial and error for a dancer to find the right shoe.

Generally, dancers with very high insteps prefer a stiffer sole to help support their feet. Dancers like myself whose arches curve towards the ends of their feet rather than higher in the ankle prefer a softer sole to facilitate standing over their toes. And dancers who had flat arches (there are no such dancers today) depended on even softer soles to prevent falling backwards off their toes altogether. As different as various American and British brands can be, the differences are subtle compared to Russian-made shoes. The underside of the toe or box end was stiffened to rigidity, making rolling through the ball of the foot (essential in smooth landings) both from pointe and jumps, extremely difficult. Russian dancers seemed to manage, but I wondered if the effort stressed their Achilles tendons. Not dancing in one's own shoes can feel treacherous, akin to walking with one's eyes closed or swimming in unchartered waters.

Moscow airport. (Left to right) Marina (Russian translator), Suzanne Hammons, Valentina (Russian translator) the author, and Bob Kauffman (company pianist), December 1963. (From the collection of Marie Paquet-Nesson)

On the morning of the fourteenth, the sets, costumes, rehearsal scores, and pointe shoes had arrived, sending a blessed wave of relief throughout the company. The appearance of Paul and me further contributed to the elation, albeit far less.

The rehearsal day was long, beginning with locating our assigned dressing rooms. Choosing individual dressing tables was up to each dancer. Claimed first were the tables at the far ends. They provided more space and a greater sense of privacy than those in the middle of a row. We rummaged through our theater cases. Souvenir trinkets joined leotards and shoes, ribbons and thread, hairpieces and rubber bands, Kleenex and tape, and the indispensable fishing tackle boxes. Fishing tackle boxes were perfect for make-up. Compartments and trays made for fishing lures, hooks, and weights were well suited for pink, orange, brown, black, white, and red pastes, tubes, and powders.

We rehearsed each ballet with many starts and stops before Bob was satisfied enough to begin the full dress rehearsal. Even though I had danced on raked stages with ABT, this was different. Adjusting to a raked stage as a solo dancer was more difficult than that as a corps dancer. In Ballet Theatre it was the stars who fretted and worried about their turns and balances, but in the Joffrey, since solo work was more or less evenly divided among about half of the company, there were many of us who fretted and worried. Except for Paul and me, the company had been working in a studio with a floor raked to the same degree as the stage. Although I bemoaned the loss of those rehearsals, the dress rehearsal progressed reasonably well.

Between class and rehearsal, and later after make-up and before our warming up again, we gathered at the canteen to rest. Feet propped on chairs and tables, we ate yogurt, black bread, and caviar and drank pear flavored soft drinks and tea, tea, and more tea.

As late afternoon approached, we were relieved to finally prepare for the evening's performance. This was a certain antidote to nervous energy. Absorbed by the orderly routine each dancer—whether quiet, giddy, serene, or animated—was totally focused on each step that took her closer to "curtain."

The most difficult ballet and the only solo role I would dance that evening was the "Pas de Deux" in *Palace*. Doing it at the end of the program (after having been in three other ballets) made it more difficult. Each ballet required a different dance style and each ballet required different shoes, reflecting the style and/or technical difficulty.

My toes began the evening comfortably spread out in black, low-heeled character shoes for *Feast*, as we continued to call it. During the second ballet, *Gamelan*, my feet along with the Flamenco inspired movements of the first ballet were strictly reigned in. Upturned hand movements in *Gamelan* suggested traditional dances from the Far East. Its simple choreography resembled less the strong lines of a wood block print than, due to velvety transitions, floating shapes of a fine watercolor. I chose my oldest pointe shoes for *Gamelan*. They were strong enough for the steps required of me. This was the last use I would get from them before throwing them out and replacing them with the shoes I was currently wearing for *Time* (or *Dawn of Humanity*). These shoes were newer, harder, and stronger to support the more vigorous leaping runs on pointe.

My newest and best shoes were saved for the most important role of the evening. Although I liked a softer arch, I wanted the box (toe end) of the shoe to be brand-new hard. I broke in my shoes by walking backstage on my toes, a minimal procedure by any standard. Staying on my toes, I flexed each foot before stepping. After a dozen steps, I would feel my weight comfortably balanced on the tips of the shoes. Only then would I practice a few ballet steps.

Other dancers liked the boxes of their shoes more broken in and wore them in class or rehearsal before wearing them on stage. A few even liked their shoes soft. Backstage, a banging sound meant that some one was hammering the undersides of the boxes. With ruthless precision, the shoe would come crashing down upon a hard surface. Cement was preferred. Holding and carefully pressing the box in a door jam was another popular technique.

Inherent in the process of changing into costumes, hairstyles, and shoes is the emotional transition from one role to the next. From a Loose Woman in *Feast* to the embodiment of the musical sounds in *Gamelan* to a predatory sexual creature in *Time* to the exotic ballerina in *Palace*, the fifteen-minute intermissions seemed, to a Joffrey bus tour veteran, almost leisurely.

During those early one-night-stand tours, the stage manager chastised us if we were not ready after a very short five-minute intermission. We performed principally in small cities and towns. It was feared that our neophyte audiences might become restless and, presumably, leave if they had to wait much longer than five minutes.

On our Harkness/State Department sponsored tours, it was a luxury to have enough time not only to change but also to practice a few steps and feel mentally composed before the curtain went back up. I forced myself to resist compulsively practicing a step about which I was nervous. The success or failure of that last practiced turn or balance could make me either satisfied or alarmed. Trying to erase the memory of a just completed splat of a turn or collapse of a balance was not a good way to begin a performance.

And then, coming from the mythical heavens above the Acropolis, was Terpsichore, the ancient Muse of Dance. To be touched by her hand meant that not only did I not have fears, falls, or missteps, but also that I would be carried effortlessly and perfectly into a harmony of music and movement. These bestowed, ecstatic experiences are rare but they are why dancers dance. Dancers begin every performance with the hope of such a Terpsichorean visit.

Bob Joffrey could be confident that, having instilled in us an exhaustive work ethic and a fierce esprit de corps, we would overcome all difficulties including a raked stage. As an added boost, on that opening night at the Mariinsky Theater, Terpsichore was, at the very least, hovering over us.

The Joffrey Ballet was a company of only twenty-six dancers. American Ballet Theatre had forty-five dancers and New York City Ballet had sixty-three. This was the Joffrey's seventh year, American Ballet Theatre had celebrated its twenty-eighth anniversary, and New York City Ballet its eighteenth. The Soviets had two major companies, The Bolshoi in Moscow and the Kirov in Leningrad. In addition, many cities throughout the Republics had their own state supported companies. Ballet was a popular and popularly priced entertainment. Audiences were knowledgeable and appreciative.

I am not dismissing the talent of the Joffrey Ballet or the valuable contribution of the Muse of Dance by suggesting that our relative inexperience may have worked in our favor. However, it may have been easy for the Soviet audiences to embrace a small, young company that was completely different than their own, both in size and stature. In addition, our entire repertoire was unfamiliar and most of the ballets were contemporary. Audiences cheered each of our ballets.

Some of the dance critics, however, viewed our more contemporary pieces through a Soviet political and social prism and, thereby, made interpretations and saw omissions that were never intended by the choreographers. Two of these were the Alvin Ailey and Brian MacDonald ballets.

Feast of Ashes, although inspired by the play of the same name, emphasized the complex interrelationships within the drama rather than the social and political upheavals. The reviewer, reminding her readers that Federico García Lorca, the author, had been killed by fascists in 1936, stated that the choreographer had not highlighted the play's social problems and that the ballet was, therefore, "impoverished." She also wrote that the "deliberate abstract dance" movements contributed to the viewer's "impression of incompleteness." I had no doubt that Alvin Ailey's only interest was in the fraught interplay between the play's characters and that he gave no thought at all to the political background of the story.

Time Out of Mind was criticized for the "exaggeratedly naturalistic" movements that turned the "chasteness of an ancient myth about sacred springtime" into something erotic and far from a "folk legend." Perhaps the Russian program notes accompanying the new Russian title spoke of myth and folk legend to put Soviet puritanical sensibilities at ease. The dancers certainly never considered the ballet to be anything other than a primitive mating ritual.

On the other hand, the same reviewer praised Bob's *Gamelan* for its adherence to the principles of classical dance and called the ballet a "stylistically subtle choreographic poem." I had no argument with that.

Throughout our tour—as far as I know—the Soviet critics had only positive things to say about the dancers. We were called young and gifted. Among the men who were singled out were Gerald Arpino, Nels Jorgensen, Paul Sutherland, and Lawrence Rhodes. Among the women were Lisa Bradley, Suzanne Hammons, Lone Isaksen, Margaret Mercier, Brunilda Ruiz, and me. But it was Lisa Bradley with her perfect body and waif-like beauty that electrified audiences and critics alike. There were two stars of the Joffrey Ballet, the Joffrey Ballet as a whole and Lisa.

A third star may have been Gerald Arpino who was not only hailed as a dramatic dancer as the Blind Man in *Pastorale*, but in his new role as choreographer. Three of his ballets were performed: *Ropes* with music by Charles Ives, *Sea Shadow* with music commissioned by Michael Colgrass (closely following the adagio movement of Ravel piano concerto in G), and *Incubus* with music by Anton Webern. Jerry had also choreographed most of the segments in *Palace*. *Palace* was a big hit. The audiences found it to be light and amusing and they loved it. Performing it as our closing piece on opening night, the audience applauded for twenty minutes. Bob, Jerry, and Konstantin Sergeyev, Director of the Kirov Ballet, joined the dancers on stage. Mr. Sergeyev said that ours was one of the most thrilling performances that he had seen. We were flushed with excitement. We were relieved and happy. "The performance went pretty well, a good dress rehearsal," I would write to my parents.

The next day the company moved to the Len-Soviet Theater where we danced eight sold out performances. "Closing night in Leningrad was very exciting," I wrote to my parents a second time, "Flowers were thrown on stage and people shouted. We had twenty-seven curtain calls."

Chapter 22

TEARS

"Mapu, Mapu, that's my new name," I joked. One of our Russian programs was being passed around. As we waited for dinner, we looked for our names in the unfamiliar Russian Cyrillic alphabet.

Seated four or six at a table in one of the Astoria Hotel's large dining rooms, we ate as a group. We never patronized the restaurants reserved for the general Soviet public and they never dined with us. Our Soviet hosts, I believed, strove to serve us meals that we would enjoy and would compare favorably with American fare. Even considering that American kitchens were stocked with American cheese, iceberg lettuce, Jello, and canned fruit, Soviet cuisine came up short. The exception was Chicken Kiev, a deep-fried breaded breast of chicken that, when pierced with a fork, gushed melted butter. It was served with potatoes and bread and more butter. All that protein, starch, and fat seemed to keep hungry dancers going well into the next day. More often, we were served patties of meat whose origins were subjected to wild speculation causing revulsion among the faint of heart and stomach.

"Mapu," I said again. The "M" and "A" of Marie looked like our own alphabet. The "R" was printed as "P" and the "E" sound was printed as "U." I quickly found my name again and again until I came to the cast of *The Palace*. "MAP" the name began, it did not finish with "U" but several other letters. "This is not my name!" I said with alarm. "There's been a mistake. The program says Margaret."

All programs, along with their casting, had been sent to the Soviet Union months in advance; this could not have been printing error. Bob must have originally cast two other dancers for the "Pas de Deux Orientale" and it was their names that had been given to Goskoncert (the booking company) for printing.

By the time Bob had begun choreographing the pas de deux, the partner who was to dance with Margaret had left the company. Bob replaced him with Paul and instead of keeping Margaret in the role, he overcame whatever initial reluctance he may have had and gave me the part instead. I should have rejoiced in Bob's faith in my technique and artistry but instead I was hurt at being second choice.

The company agreed to make announcements of the cast change and true to its word, each of the many times *The Palace* was performed, a Soviet spokesman stepped out in front of the curtain. Costumed and ready to dance, Paul and I anticipated the audience's hushed attention as the theater official appeared. It was rather grand to hear our names announced into the theaters of Leningrad, Donetsk, Kharkov, Kiev, and Moscow. We were happy and it did partially compensate for the disappointment.

Because Soviet officials held all passports, birthday celebrations organized by our hosts during the eight-week tour were inescapable. Mine, coming at the end of our third and last week in Leningrad was the first and, therefore, a surprise. "A birthday toast," said one of our interpreters as we sat down for a late October meal. Our glasses were filled with vodka and everyone drank to my success and the furthering of American/Soviet relations. I was given a box of very waxy and very sweet chocolates. Bob had slipped out of the room during the toast and returned carrying a small gift. Wrapped in rough, gray packing paper provided by the hotel gift shop, it made a faint thud as he set it down in front of me. It was a shiny, lacquered, paper mache box. Hand painted from the village of Mstera, the traditional Russian fairy tale "The Maiden with the Golden Hair" was painted in intricate detail. Using single-haired brushes and a magnifying glass, the princess, her attendants, the prince, and his decorated horses had been painted in dazzling color. Bob gave gifts less frequently than he gave complements. Although Bob was always polite and, on occasion, unexpectedly funny, he was not overly affectionate. The gift, I knew, meant that he thought of me with fondness. I kept his gift cradled in its own niche in my make-up box. It held my rhinestone stage earrings. Today, it sits on a bedroom shelf. It holds a single dried rose.

Birthdays always made me feel a year older than the younger dancers and stirred up thoughts of one year less to dance. Generally, only the more successful ballet dancers perform past the age of thirty and only a handful dance to forty and beyond. The oldest dancers usually know enough to take themselves out of the more technically demanding roles. Creaky joints, tight tendons, and stiff muscles make the technique more difficult and increase the risk of injury.

One dancer, in the title role in Eugene Loring's *Billy the Kid*, performed a few years too many. Over the course of the ballet, Billy shot six men. With each shot Aaron Copeland's music and the choreography rose to a fevered pitch. With aerial spins and a landing into a forward leaning pose, Billy killed each of his rivals. He was dressed in tights, chaps, boots, shirt, and a holster. Quite convincingly, his hand mimicked a gun. After each killing, and in silence, he returned his mimed gun to its holster and, still in silence, did a ritualized slow motion walk symbolizing some combination of stealth, revulsion, and bravado. The ballet, although an effective abstraction of reality, suffered from this dancer's lost balon (bounce in landing from a jump). The easy spring of a tennis ball is ideal; a thump is not acceptable. When an audience's eye is unintentionally jarred, the ballet's believability is on the line. It is embarrassing to watch a fine dancer dance too long.

I stopped dancing at age thirty. My personal experience with the ballet body rearing up with a mighty "whoa" happened not on stage but in the classroom while teaching. On a hot and humid day, a condition friendly to dancers' limbs and spines, I was demonstrating an arabesque, my leg lifted to the back. My body felt more limber than usual. Chest lifted, back erect, eyes wide and expressive, arms held delicately in the prescribed Russian pedagogical third arabesque position, I was sure that my back leg, long and still lean enough, had lifted to an impressive ninety-degree angle off the floor. Surely, the only thing wanting in this arabesque was the Swan Queen's tutu and feathered headpiece. My back padlocked into position and I confidently looked at myself in the mirror. "Where is my leg?" I thought for a millisecond. My eyes scanned down the surface of the mirror to my leg. And there it was, only twenty-four inches off the floor. Dancers know how high their back legs are lifted by the strength of the muscles just above and below the waist. The higher the leg, the more strongly the muscles engage except for older and/or out of shape dancers. On that memorable summer day, the familiar clench in the back simply meant that the leg was lifted. It ceased to be a reliable gauge of height.

However, four years earlier in 1963, I was celebrating my twenty-sixth birthday. My jump had balon and my arabesque muscles worked well, but I was tired to the core. We did as many as eight performances a week and I danced in three or four ballets each performance. "I have no time at all and my free days are spent sleeping and washing. That is all," I wrote to my parents. My weight had dropped from one hundred and ten pounds to one hundred and five. I had no physical or emotional reserve. However, I also wrote, "The company continues to be very well received and I feel as though I have danced well."

The trip from Leningrad to Donetsk, the first of three Ukrainian cities we visited, took twenty-four hours. Familiar were the big red stars on the exterior of the train, the nineteenth century ambiance of the interiors, and the "tea lady." Sharing the compartment with another couple and dissecting company gossip with them shortened the long ride. There had been rumors coursing through hotel and backstage hallways that—even considering that the company had risen to its greatest success—trouble was brewing. Was it true that Mrs. Harkness wanted to weigh in on decisions relating to hiring dancers, choosing repertoire, and, God forbid, selecting music for new ballets? Was it true that she wanted the Robert Joffrey Ballet to be renamed something generic like the American National Ballet or, worse, The Harkness Ballet? Surely, Bob would not let this happen. Surely, Bob was in control. Bob's company was his company, the fruition of his and Gerald Arpino's dream. Surely, any problems would be resolved. In January 1964, a month after our scheduled return from the Soviet Union, another States tour had been planned under the sponsorship of Joffrey's former presenter, Columbia Artists Management, Inc., not the Rebekah W. Harkness Foundation. What did this mean? None of us liked to think about bus tours. Surely, the company had matured past those grueling one-night-stand tours.

Retreating from problems and avoiding confrontation seemed to be Bob Joffrey's way of coping with stress. The dancers, and especially his more senior dancers, felt as though Bob was retreating from them personally. Leaving most company classes and rehearsals to the ballet master, Richard Thomas, Bob spent increasingly less time with us, his company. We had been sustained by his expertise, optimism, and intensity. His critical eye assured our progress as artists. Now it seemed as though he did not care.

Our ballet master, Richard Thomas (father of the actor Richard Thomas), had been a dancer with the New York City Ballet and was a popular teacher among current New York professionals. From his Balanchine influence, his classes emphasized clearly defined and speedy footwork, important attributes in Balanchine's choreography. Concerned, also, that his students execute particularly complex and strenuous exercises with a relaxed aplomb, he would put us at ease by choosing the most tense among us and begin a conversation about something totally unrelated, such as the weather. It was difficult to both struggle and giggle. I liked him and found his classes valuable, but not on a tour where the weather was cold, the theaters were cool, and my muscles were sore from overwork. We needed slow warm-ups, not challenges in speed. Bob's classes were perfect and we missed them. We could not understand his choice of ballet master. With every cramped calf muscle, dissatisfaction grew.

But for now, the customary round of classes, rehearsals, and performances reclaimed our thoughts and energies. We were the first foreign performance group of any kind to have come to Donetsk, a Ukrainian mining town of nine hundred thousand people. Within three days of the announcement of our performances, all twelve hundred seats for each of the six performances had been sold.

We were in Donetsk on November 7, Revolution Day, during a three-day holiday. Military hardware and brass must have been amassed for grand displays in the major cities because the parade in Donetsk was a "People's Demonstration."

Large groups from housing projects, schools, and mining collectives marched by the reviewing stand that was flanked by outsized portraits of Lenin. Only a few elderly folk and the Joffrey dancers were left on the sidelines to watch the colorful flags, floats, and banners go by.

Clamorous applause closed our week in Donetsk. The next day we boarded a bus for Kharkov—the second largest city (after Kiev)—in the Ukraine. Since before the revolution of 1917 Kharkov was known as one of the world's leading mathematics centers. It was also where the Germans had their last strategic victory in World War II.

The pain of the war, less than twenty years before, was not far from the minds of everyone we talked to. About sixty percent (3.3 million) of the Soviet POWs had died by the end of the war. This contrasted to about four percent of American and British POWs; this reflected, perhaps, the Nazi belief that Americans and British were racially equal to themselves. Soviets, on the other hand, were considered not only subhuman but also a Bolshevik menace, a Jewish conspiracy menace. Second to the Jews, Soviet citizens were the largest group to be victimized by Nazi racial policy. As a result, perhaps, the Russians I spoke with told me that life was relatively good, the dearth of consumer goods and any lack of freedoms were temporary, and life was getting better. I wrote to my parents, "Soviet citizens seem to be Russians first. Communism is their way of life. From scanty outward appearances, people seem happy, enthusiastic, and proud."

It has been said that the Soviet roads had halted the German advance. They did not stop the Joffrey Company. (We were lucky, I was told, that it was neither snowing nor raining.) The one-hundred and fifty miles to Kharkov from Donetsk took a long and bumpy seven hours. Along the way we stopped at a cluster of several one-story buildings, literally, in the middle of nowhere. The community toilet facility was memorable. "Worse than what I remember from small towns in Spain and India and believe me, that's bad," I reported back home. "The Russians should forget about reaching the moon and I know just how some of those rubles could be spent." I was shocked at the primitive conditions around me. Our Russian interpreters and officials looked embarrassed and I had no doubt that traveling to our next destination, Kiev, would not be by bus. However, the enthusiasm and warmth with which we were greeted throughout our week in Kharkov made the Spartan trek worthwhile.

From Kharkov we flew, thank God, into Kiev, one of the oldest cities in Eastern Europe. As with each of our opening night performances, this one, on November 22, 1963, was a glorious success. Back at the recently built Moskva Hotel (today the Ukrayina) we hurried towards the dining room when we were stopped and called into a separate room. The door closed behind us. A Soviet official, ashen and agitated, spoke. "President Kennedy has died," he said. I turned to my friends. "He's wrong. He means Joseph Kennedy." Everyone knew that the president's elderly father had been sick. The heavily accented voice, commanding but gentle, was continuing, "President Kennedy has been assassinated."

John Kennedy had been shot while we were performing. JFK, for whom we had just danced six weeks previously, with whom we had shook hands, was dead. It was six weeks since I had been awed by the splendor and history of the East Room, the place where Lincoln had lain-in-state. John Kennedy would lie-in-state in the same room, within a few feet from where we had danced.

I put my hands over my face. Eyes covered, I became aware of the sounds in the room. Framed in silence, they came at random from corner to back wall, from close by, and further away. There were gasps, sighs, questions, and sobs that were both stifled and deep throated.

Our performances were canceled until after the President's funeral, three days hence. A first for Soviet television, programs were interrupted. Hand-held announcements were read. Blank screens and organ music replaced all programming. Our friends and families back home were held hostage in front of their television sets for three days. There was no satellite transmission in 1963, so we would see none of the black and white funeral footage that would be forever imprinted into history. We felt isolated.

Viewed as symbols of pre-revolutionary repression, all churches had been closed for over forty years. Thanks to Bob's intercession, the bells from onion domed St. Vladimir's peeled and doors were opened. Hundreds of Russian Orthodox Ukrainians joined the company for a memorial service. As in all Russian Orthodox churches, attendees stood during the service. There were no pews. Mosaics and frescoes flickered from a galaxy of candles. Bearded priests, robed in Byzantine splendor, intoned chants and prayers. Members of the Kiev Opera joined in the choir. "Everyone was crying," reported a friend. I had not attended the service; I could not bear the sorrow.

Instead, I left the hotel for a long aimless walk. Our hotel was part of the post war reconstruction in central Kiev. Around Maidan Nezalezhnosti or Independence Square (site of the Orange Revolution) was the same large neo-classical Stalinist architecture, which was typical of all the country's post-revolution buildings. What they lacked in charm, they made up for in bulky size. The grouping that included the Central Post Office and the Trade Union House with its high-rise clock sent a message of stolid permanence. In the center of the square were fountains.

Closing night in Moscow. Curtain call for The Palace. (Front row/left to right) Christine Sarry, Virginia Stuart, Suzanne Hammons, Nancy Fenster, the author (in harem pants), Lisa Bradley, Brunilda Ruiz, Margaret Mercier, Carina Rieger, Marlene Rizzo (head turned), and Noel Mason. (Back row/left to right) Helgi Tomasson, Paul Sutherland (in turban), Felix Smith, John Wilson, Lawrence Rhodes, Robert Vickery, Nels Jorgensen, James Howell, and Yuri Krasnopolsky (the Joffrey conductor), December 1963. (From the collection of Suzanne Hammons-Daone)

I watched the water spring up and listened to it splash into a pool. I stood there for a long time. Walking slowly along Khreschatyk (Kiev's main street) I was conspicuously dressed in a Saks Fifth Avenue jacket. Hip-length and fur-trimmed it kept me warm and, on that day, comforted. (Mrs. Harkness had bought each of the women identical jackets and each of the men different, identical jackets.)

I passed many people that morning and wondered if they always looked that somber. "Maybe I am seeing my own dark mood reflected back at me," I thought. "Could it be that they and I are burdened by a shared grief?"

An old woman was walking directly into my path. She stopped. As I looked into her pale blue eyes she said something that I did not understand, but I nodded slightly. We both knew that I did not understand and it did not matter. She reached into her thickly padded double-breasted coat and pulled out a piece of newspaper. Turning her palm towards me, she revealed what she had been keeping inside her coat. It was a picture of John F. Kennedy. The grieving was, indeed, shared.

The day after President Kennedy's funeral and the Russian memorial service, we were back in the theater for our second and final performance of what was supposed to have been a full week of performances. In Moscow, our next city and the last of the tour, we danced to thirteen sold out performances in ten days. Bob Joffrey, in front of the curtain, dedicated the opening night to President Kennedy. He assured the audience that President Johnson would continue the policies of the Kennedy era.

On our closing night in Moscow the company took thirty-four curtain calls. Nothing would ever be the same again.

Chapter 23

Two Companies

In early December 1963, The Joffrey Company was back in New York City and in January we were in Los Angeles, finishing the first half of the cross-country bus tour. It was here that our careers abruptly changed. Flying in from New York, Jeannot Cerrone, the company manager, surprised us with his visit and his call for a company meeting.

Waiting for the meeting to begin I thought of the many times Bob spoke to his dancers, all thirteen and, then, all twenty of us. Happily huddled in his small office, we listened to his plans for the company. We caught his hopes and enthusiasm and, carrying them into rehearsals and classes, attempted to match his unbridled energy from the first plié to the last rehearsal of the day. This meeting would be different. To begin with, Bob was not in attendance.

Jeannot began speaking. Mrs. Harkness would be starting her own company, he told us, and it would be called The Harkness Ballet. Bob had been offered the position of artistic director but because he had not responded, someone else had been hired (George Skibine, former ballet master of the Paris Opera Ballet). New contracts would be offered to those dancers who chose to stay; those who chose not to would be released from their current contracts. All the ballets (and their sets and costumes) that had been choreographed under Harkness sponsorship would now belong to the new company. Bob would be allowed to keep his *Gamelan* and all of Jerry Arpino's ballets. The Joffrey repertoire prior to Harkness would also remain with Bob. Although we knew that problems between Bob and Mrs. Harkness had been mounting, we were shocked by the news.

Dancers are usually well outside the sphere of management, but even so, we were aware of some of Mrs. Harkness's unwelcome artistic involvement. She had successfully vetoed the inclusion of Anna Sokolow's *Perspectives* (one of the Watch Hill ballets) into the company's repertoire. It was rumored that she hated both the choreographer and her ballet. And, of course, we all knew of her interest in seeing her own music brought to choreographic life. Had Bob taken the artistic directorship job, I had no doubt that his artistic power would have been curtailed and his vision of the company's future thwarted. Bob was the very heart of the Joffrey Ballet. I considered its being renamed the Harkness Ballet blasphemy. We had heard that changing the name of the company to The Harkness Ballet was the requirement imposed by the Harkness Foundation in order to secure its continued financial support of the Joffrey Ballet. However, many believed that this was the legal justification for Mrs. Harkness's desire to take over ownership of the Joffrey Ballet.

Where was Bob? Why was he not around? Where was he? Why had he not spoken to us? We knew that Bob avoided conflict and sometimes retreated from sight but why now? Why, when we needed to hear directly from him? The responsibilities of a larger company, as it surely had become, had been keeping him away from us as a teacher and coach. We regretted this, increasingly with bitterness, but now we were desperate to hear from him. How could we make decisions that would affect the rest of our professional lives if he did not talk to us? A couple of the original six dancers from the station wagon days telephoned him and begged him to speak to us directly. I wonder how my eventual choice might have been different if he had. The message he related to us, however, stated that because he had no work to offer us he would understand if we chose to stay with Harkness.

The choice was between Harkness with the promise of work under union conditions and Joffrey with a company in limbo and no work. Eleven of the twenty-six dancers, many of them older and more experienced, stayed with Harkness. Their careers were well established; they had bills to pay and wanted to perform. (Helgi Tomasson would soon leave Harkness Ballet for New York City Ballet.)

The Harkness Ballet would last from 1964 until 1974, when the Harkness Foundation decided that it could no longer finance the company's considerable expense. But for ten years the company performed in many of Europe's principal opera houses to mostly critical acclaim. The dancers were universally praised. One of my friends missed Bob's artistic direction. Without it, she said, her years with the company were not fulfilling. Another friend, however, reported a very different experience. She spoke of collaboration between choreographers, composers, and designers that reminded her of Diaghilev's Ballets Russe, thereby contributing to the most satisfying years of her career.

There could be no argument, however, over the sincerity and admiration that Mrs. Harkness held for her dancers. It was important for her to provide her dancers with both comfortable standards of living and regal working conditions. She purchased and renovated a town house on the East Side of Manhattan. Studios, dressing rooms, a cafeteria, offices, and a newly created school were housed in the luxury that only an upper east-side townhouse could provide. In the same spirit of appreciation—and acknowledgment of dancers' preoccupation with food, I wondered with amusement?—she had the names of the Harkness dancers stenciled along the border of the ceiling in the cafeteria.

Entering the elegant East 72nd Street townhouse, the dancers stepped into a lobby with a high, ornate ceiling and a floor of black and white marble tile. Upstairs, four large studios were referred to by their dominant colors: gray, red, peach, and blue. In the center of the blue studio ceiling was the Harkness House symbol, a dancer holding a book with leafed vines attached to his feet. A bejeweled elevator cage passed painted scenes of famous ballets. Along the winding, marble staircase and set in an alcove was a work of art designed by Salvidor Dali. Mrs. Harkness had commissioned Dali, a member of her inner circle, to make a chalice that, it was rumored, would eventually hold her ashes. Encased in bulletproof glass, the *Chalice of Life* was overlaid with small, jewel-encrusted butterflies. It sat on a rotating pedestal, and with each rotation, the butterflies opened and closed, perhaps foretelling the transmutation to come.

I preferred studios in the under-whelming old, commercial buildings of the West Side of Manhattan. In a nineteenth century starving artist romantic kind of way, I believed that the unadorned simplicity of worn wood floors, overhead florescent lights, old company photographs, and frayed posters were the necessary foundation from which great art could shine. I thought luxury was counterproductive to sweat and creativity, just as I did of the sun splashed, ocean sprayed dance facilities at Watch Hill, Rhode Island. (However, I always thought the showers were a good idea.)

Nine (some of the youngest and least experienced) dancers stayed with Bob. The six dancers who chose neither Harkness nor Bob either took jobs with other companies or retired. The new band of Joffrey dancers took classes, rehearsed, and waited. The rift between the companies aired in the press. Sympathy and help from the dance world set the groundwork for a new Joffrey Ballet which rose Phoenix-like to a grand height in 1966 when it became the resident ballet company of The City Center Theater. (The theater was originally built in 1923 as a meeting hall for the Ancient Order of the Nobles of the Mystic Shrine.)

As the home of New York City Ballet before it moved to Lincoln Center, the City Center stage had been established as a place where a sophisticated and curious New York dance audience watched their resident ballet company grow, change, and innovate. They took personal interest in the progress of their favorite dancers, looked forward to new ballets, and returned time and again as loyal fans. A rapport developed between the people who walked through the neo Moorish facade on

56th Street and the dancers who passed through the 55th Street stage door. Each put the street and their everyday lives behind them with the expectation of becoming connected by a performance that, on special occasions, was a common, exalted experience.

The Joffrey was uniquely qualified to step onto the City Center stage. As a medium-sized theater with limited backstage areas, it was perfectly suited for the shorter and smaller ballets which Bob's company presented. The intimacy of viewing smaller ballets is enhanced by a theater and stage that are also smaller in scale. City Center would never have been able to accommodate the palaces required for *Sleeping Beauty* and *Swan Lake* and other full-scale productions for which other companies, including American Ballet Theatre, were principally known. (Today, ABT has two performing seasons in New York: one at Lincoln Center for full-scale productions and a second one at City Center for their smaller ballets.) I can only imagine how happy Bob was to agree to his new company name, The City Center Joffrey Ballet.

In ten years, from 1966 until 1976, The City Center Joffrey Ballet grew in size, scope, and importance. Bob was a lover of all dance and intensely interested in dance history. His company was in the perfect city, the perfect theater, and the perfect decades to embody that history. The Joffrey presented mid-twentieth century masterpieces from established, major European choreographers not in American repertoires as well as groundbreaking, cutting edge ballets that stretched into popular culture. The company was also unprecedented in presenting ballets from the past, not full length, nineteenth century ballets like *Swan Lake*, but rarely seen and even lost ballets from the early twentieth century Diaghilev era such as *Le Sacre Du Printemps*.

Diaghilev was a Russian visionary, art historian, and impresario. His Parisian-based, early twentieth century Ballets Russe brought early Modernist visual art, music, and dance into legendary, innovative, and, sometimes, controversial collaborations. Among these collaborations were Michel Fokine's *Petrouchka* with music and libretto by Stravinsky and costumes by Benois (first performed in 1911); Massine's *Parade* with music by Satie, libretto by Cocteau and costumes by Picasso (first performed in 1917); Massine's *Le Tricorne* with music by de Falla and costumes by Picasso (first performed in 1919); Massine's *Pulcinella* with music by Stravinsky and costumes by Picasso (first performed in 1920); Bronislava Nijinska's (Vaslav Nijinsky's sister) *Les Noces* with music and text by Stravinsky and costumes by Goncharova (first performed in 1923); Nijinsky's *L'Apres-Midi D'un Faune* with music by Debussy and costumes by Bakst (first performed in 1912);

and Nijinsky's *Le Sacre Du Printemps*, music by Igor Stravinsky and concept and costume design by Nicolas Roerich.

Since there were very few performances of *Le Sacre Du Printemps* after its 1913 Paris premiere, Bob's dance researchers found its reconstruction a particular challenge. It took years of work, travel, and research by dance historian Millicent Hodson and art historian Kenneth Archer (working on costume and set designs) to piece together the ballet. They gathered sketches, photographs, and paintings contemporary to the time along with choreographic notes on Stravinsky's original score and interviews with people who had seen the ballet. Ms. Hodson filled in choreography to connect passages. The effort culminated in a 1987 production about which Bob would be particularly proud. The Joffrey audience roared its approval. (This was a very different reaction from the 1913 audience that, famously, nearly caused a riot. The audience shouted and booed so ferociously that Stravinsky left the seat where he had been sitting for the safety of backstage. He found Nijinsky in the wings, yelling counts over the bedlam so that the dancers could keep track of what they were doing.)

The Joffrey was the first American company to perform *The Green Table*, a ballet whose stature and reputation as an anti war statement has been mythic almost from its inception. Choreographed by Kurt Jooss in 1932 and performed by Ballets Jooss (the choreographer's own company based in Germany), it had been entered in a choreographic competition in Paris. Winning first place, it attained international success but also serious criticism back in Germany. Kurt Jooss had refused to let go of his Jewish dancers or the commissioned composer for the ballet, Frederic Cohen. Instead, the entire company left (or perhaps more accurately, escaped) Germany for a number of different countries, England and Chile among them.

Coincidently, the parents of one of the Joffrey dancers, Michael Uthoff, had been in the original production and from this connection *The Green Table* began an American life as it brought its timely anti-war message to the Joffrey's 1967 audience. It was the company's great fortune that Kurt Jooss came to New York and oversaw the final rehearsal details. (Today the ballet remains in the repertoire of The Joffrey Ballet of Chicago.)

The ballet takes its name from a long green table that is tipped slightly downwards towards the audience making the surface easily visible. The table, starkly lit on a dim stage, seemed to garishly slice the space, perhaps symbolically representing one of war's many wounds. The first and last scenes are identical. Diplomats, dressed in formal black with white spats and white gloves and wearing white German Expressionist masks, face off across the table. They gesture, pound, and debate in repetitive and ritualistic movements. They accomplish nothing, giving the ballet its unfortunate timeless relevancy. Although all the characters are indispensable, the main character is Death Stalking. A list of some of the rest of the cast tells the story: Standard Bearer, Young Soldier, Young Girl, Old Soldier, Guerilla Woman, Old Woman, and Profiteer.

Suzanne Hammons—the only dancer to have first made the Harkness choice and then return to Bob's company—performed the Guerilla Woman role. Since Suzanne and I did some of the same roles in the "old" Joffrey company, I watched her reentry into the Joffrey Ballet with particular interest.

I also enjoyed seeing classical ballets only rarely seen by American audiences at City Center. Sir Frederick Ashton from England's Royal Ballet and John Cranko the British director of the Stuttgart Ballet were among the great twentieth century European classical ballet choreographers. The Joffrey presented *Façade* from 1931; *Wedding Bouquet* and *Les Patineurs* from 1937; *Illuminations* from 1950; *Monotones I & II* from 1965; *Jazz Calendar* from 1968; and *The Dream*, a one act ballet based on *A Midsummer Night's Dream*, from 1973. John Cranko's prolific career was represented by an early work, *Pineapple Poll* from 1951, and two of his full evening ballets based on Shakespearean plays, *Romeo and Juliet* from 1962 and *Taming of the Shrew* from 1969. John Cranko had an uncanny ability to tell complex stories without pantomime. His corps de ballet crowd scenes, whether depicting noblemen and women or robust peasants, were choreographically intricate and engaging. They were more likely to hold the interest of uninitiated audiences that, while watching similar scenes in the old nineteenth century classics, might become impatient until the story line and "real" dancing restarted.

From the time of Alvin Ailey's *Feast of Ashes* (that remained with Harkness Ballet) and Anna Sokolow's piece (that never saw the light of day), Bob's interest in incorporating modern dance works, including commissioned pieces, was yet another facet of his encompassing reach. He hired many modern dance choreographers including John Butler, Laura Dean, Stuart Hodes, Jose Limon, Paul Taylor, Glen Tetley, Twyla Tharp, and again, Alvin Ailey and Anna Sokolow.

Twyla Tharp's commissioned *Deuce Coupe* was choreographed to music of the Beach Boys. It was the first of many works she would eventually choreograph for ballet companies and on ballet dancers. (Her own company employed ballet dancers and her ballet master was Jonathon Watts, an early Joffrey dancer and New York City Ballet principal dancer.) In an interview for the Academy of Achievement (a museum of living history established in 1961 in Washington, D.C.), Twyla Tharp talks about how Bob took a real leap of faith. "Back then, everyone thought that ballet and modern dance were separate," she said. "Walls are unhealthy things." She choreographed additional ballets for the Joffrey Ballet before choreographing the celebrated *Push Comes to Shove* for Mikhail Baryshnikov at ABT, using music from both Mozart and Scott Joplin.

I never imagined that Bob would choreograph a ballet that would be described as "cutting edge," much less featured on the cover of *Time Magazine*. But he did and it did. *Astarte* was the first multimedia rock ballet to be performed by a ballet company. Anxious to create the biggest possible impact, the two dancers involved not only knew little about the production during initial rehearsals, but when they did, they were sworn to secrecy. Trinette Singleton, her forehead decorated with a lotus flower and her body covered in a henna-like, all-over, paisley patterned unitard, danced the role of Astarte, an ancient goddess of fertility. She performed the role with charismatic qualities that intermingled steel and gossamer. Her partner, Maximillo Zomosa, matched her charisma with his over six-foot height and magnetic sexuality. As if to emphasize his role as a mortal being, the ballet began with him sitting, fully dressed, in the audience. After being searched out by a spotlight, he stood up, walked to the side of the stage, up a few steps and moved toward center stage. He removed his clothes and stood there in his briefs. A mutual seduction ensued. At the ballet's conclusion, Astarte disappeared and the backdrop lifted to reveal City Center's back brick wall lined with heating pipes and an opened rear stage door. The male dancer, still in his briefs, walked out of the door to a clearly visible 55th Street beyond.

The ballet was sensational in 1967. The audience had been further stunned by the loud rock music commissioned by Crome Syrcus and by a huge, silken, billowing backdrop. A black-and-white film of the dancers, many times larger than life, had been created and shot by Gardner Compton. The dancers were filmed performing the same choreography that they would perform live on stage. Sometimes the images were synchronized and sometimes they were not.

Jerry Arpino was interested in social issues. The *Clowns* from 1968 made a dramatic antinuclear statement beginning with the opening sounds from Hershy Kay's commissioned score. An aural blast of exploding atomic bombs was followed by the tumbling fall of clowns (life sized dolls) from the rafters of the stage. Landing amidst a cloud of white dust, one dancer/clown emerges as the only survivor. *Trinity*, from 1970 with music from Alan Rath and Lee Holdridge, was another anti-war ballet. Long gone were the earlier days when my contemporaries and I worked pretty much in seclusion from current social and political issues. *Trinity*, choreographed while the Vietnam war was still churning to its tragic conclusion, not only spoke to society's discontented youth but also it was performed by dancers who, themselves, were members of the same counterculture.

The following composers are a partial listing that indicates the scope of Gerald Arpino's choreography. Beginning with a ballet using music by Anton Webern in 1962 and continuing through over two decades, Jerry has used music by Vivaldi, Toshiro Mayuzumi, John LaMontaine, Mozart, Rossini, Tchaikovsky, Jacob Druckman, Johann Strauss, Johann Simon Mayer, Emmanuel Chabrier, Stephen Foster, Saint-Saens, Shostakovich, Douglas Adams, Russ Gauthier, and Mahler.

In 1975, The City Center of Music and Drama reorganized. Although the Joffrey Ballet continued performing at City Center, it was no longer the resident company and therefore, financial support was limited. As a result, a year later, the company dropped City Center from its name and once again the Joffrey Ballet was called The Joffrey Ballet. Then in 1983, and continuing for eight years, the Joffrey became bi-coastal as the resident ballet company of The Music Center of Los Angeles, performing both at the Dorothy Chandler Pavilion in Los Angeles and at the City Center in New York.

On March 25, 1988, everything stopped. A jolt went through the dance world, the company, and many hearts. After a long illness, at the age of fifty-nine years, Robert Joffrey died. Jerry's role as (former) dancer, choreographer, advisor, and confidante would now include company director.

However, shortly thereafter, the board voted for a fundamental change in the structure of the company. Gerald Arpino, the artistic director, would not be given complete artistic control of the company, a control that had been specified in Bob Joffrey's will. This was the start of multiple disagreements. The Joffrey Ballet assumes a vision dictated by the board, not one born from the roots and dreams of the Joffrey/Arpino association? Unthinkable! Jerry resigned and the Los Angeles residency ended. Jerry was left with his ballets, the support of the dancers, and his undying optimism for the future.

And again, there was another reinvention. In 1995 under Jerry's leadership, the company became The Joffrey Ballet of Chicago. Chicago had long wanted a first class ballet company to call its own and Chicagoans from 1957 had always welcomed the Joffrey Ballet. (I remember the excitement of dancing on the Chicago Opera stage and the satisfaction at reading the company's good reviews. Receiving good reviews from knowledgeable critics was, after all, more rewarding than those from combined music, dance, and art critics from small town newspapers or, least impressively, those that appeared on the society page.)

Speaking of the Chicago move, Diane Haithman, *Los Angeles Times* staff writer, said in 2003, "The Chicago arts climate allowed the Joffrey to put down roots in a way that always seemed to elude the company in Los Angeles. Chicago is a tighter community, focusing on the arts, not just entertainment..." "We don't have a movie industry. And this (Chicago) is a big testing ground for Broadway, a big preview town. It's fertile ground to set up shop." Since then, the company has been mentioned as one part of a cultural triumvirate along with the Chicago Lyric Opera and the Chicago Symphony Orchestra.

The Joffrey Ballet is in Chicago, but it belongs to more than a city. The Joffrey is an American company, born from vision, talent, hard work, success, failure, more success, perseverance, and optimism—qualities I like to think are still part of the greater American fabric. In 2006, the Joffrey Ballet celebrated its fiftieth anniversary in Chicago. This American company, forty-six dancers strong, celebrated with youthful exuberance and eclectic styles, ballets of the past, ballets classical and contemporary, and a body of work from each of the two founders.

Gerald Arpino, in a 2006 interview, acknowledged that the company would have a new beginning when a new director succeeded him. "I think the legacy will be a top person, but one much more of a director than a choreographer. The person must have a knowledge of the repertory and come wanting to preserve the company's style for what it is—that is, all styles and no style." On July 1, 2007, such a director, Ashley Wheater, was chosen. Mr. Arpino was named Artistic Director Emeritus. Alas, the following year, on October 29, 2008, dear Gerald Arpino passed away.

Today the company is artistically acclaimed, on solid financial footing, and, in July 2008, moved into its new downtown Chicago home. Named the Joffrey Tower, the company relocated into forty-five-thousand square feet of space on the third and fourth floors of this new thirty-two story building. Administrative offices, seven rehearsal studios, and a black box theater will call Ten East Randolph their home. A sense of permanence is gratifying.

Having been a part of the Joffrey past, I feel connected to its future.

Chapter 24

RETIRED

Paul and I had been offered contracts with the Metropolitan Opera Ballet. The new Metropolitan Opera House at Lincoln Center had been completed. We lived nearby. Ending my career as it had begun, I would have been one of those older dancers about whom I wondered a decade ago. Back then I was in the company to get my pink satin foot into the door of Swan Queen dreams. Returning, it would have been a comfortable place to not dream before the stage door finally clicked closed. Although I was not particularly excited about rejoining the Met Opera Ballet, I was gratified not to have to make a choice between Joffrey and Harkness.

Two days before signing with the Met, American Ballet Theatre called to ask if we were interested, once again, in joining the company. We were and we did.

Although I participated in yet another lengthy States tour, a tour of Central and South America, and a third tour (my second with ABT) to the Soviet Union, those last dancing years left me with few memories. I had resigned myself to biding my time until Paul retired, after which we would pursue our vague plan to teach somewhere together.

I was content to coast easily in the corps de ballet, sparing myself the stress of competing for more challenging roles. Although I nearly always shone on stage, competing for solo parts was difficult for me both in the Joffrey and, in particular, in the much larger and more hierarchical ABT. Overcome with self-consciousness, I was not able to convince choreographers and ballet masters that I was capable of solo parts even though I knew I was—at least of some. I had depended on Bob to prod and encourage me. As the company expanded, Bob's energy had turned to greater responsibilities. It was my responsibility to take care of myself. I had been given opportunities to rediscover courage within myself both in the Joffrey and ABT. I was not psychologically prepared to do this. Instead I took on a cynical, indifferent attitude that, on one occasion, nearly got me into trouble.

I had been assigned to understudy the turning "black (tutu) girls" in *Etudes*, a ballet choreographed by the Danish choreographer, Harold Lander. The music, by

Carl Czerny, had been composed as piano practice pieces, hence the name "Etudes" (studies). It was the perfect foil for the choreographer's theatrical recreation of a ballet class. The music and the ballet began with simple exercises that gradually increased in complexity until the flashy allegro finale brought the house down.

The curtain opened with the corps women dressed in black tutus standing along barres against a backlit scrim. Starkly silhouetted like Victorian shadow images, our dancing in perfect unity was critical. Whether doing crisp battements battu (beating exercises for the feet) or languid fondues (exercises that begin with melting pliés), these familiar exercises could be terrifying. The slightest deviations in direction, timing, or coordination stood out in sharp focus.

Stretching and splits were the concluding exercises. We left the stage in darkness. The barres were removed and the lights brightened. The soloists entered and began the adagio portion of the class. They and their partners along with the principals wore white and danced in most of the subsequent sections. The "white (tutu) girls" turned; the principals did an adagio; the men did tours en l'air; the white girls did small jumps; the ballerina did a solo; the premier danseur did his; the black girls, one at a time, crisscrossed the stage with long leaps; and the entire company concluded the ballet with a jump-filled Mazurka.

One of the premier danseur's bravura moments featured multiple turns at center stage. Standing in one place and on one leg, he did a lengthy series of turns, the difficulty of which was recognized and appreciated by audiences that commenced applauding at about measure sixteen and continued through to the exultant ending pose. Turning with him were four black-tutued girls, each starting from a corner of the stage. They, including me as an understudy, did several wide circles of traveling turns around him. Midway we changed direction to turn, spoke-like in towards the still pirouetting premier danseur. Before getting too close, we again changed direction, to retrace our steps. We then circled one last time before exiting.

The first time I was called upon to do the turning section, I was neither concerned that I had not practiced the turns, nor that I was out of shape. After all, compared to some of the dancing I had done with the Joffrey the task at hand was not especially daunting. So when I took my place in the downstage right hand corner and began turning I was shocked, after only sixteen turns, to find myself feeling dizzy. And I got dizzier with each succeeding turn. Would I career over? Or more horrifyingly, would I bump into Royes Fernandez, an ABT star of whom I was particularly fond? The more I turned, the brighter the lights from the wings became. They swirled around my head. They blurred my vision. "Spot, spot, spot," I shouted to myself with each snap of the head, hoping that vertigo would not overtake me. Each spot seemed to consume every bit of energy and concentration I could muster. I made it through. I must be very out of shape, I thought.

No longer ambitiously striving for future roles and having settled for a relatively stress-free corps de ballet life, I had neither the desire nor did I see the need to remain in the peak of condition. Even as I took perverse pride in being able to dance well in my corps work without taking class regularly, I was, more appropriately, proud to have been cast in a new ballet.

It was my Joffrey experiences with modern ballets that made the casting possible. Glen Tetley, a dancer with both ballet and modern dance experience was the choreographer. Although Glen had been one of the six Joffrey dancers on the Joffrey Ballet's two station wagon tours in 1956 and 1957, I did not come to know him until 1960 when we were both in American Ballet Theatre. He had already begun to choreograph when he joined ABT as principal dancer. His work, a fusion of ballet and modern dance, would become well known in Europe and Canada where he would choreograph for many major companies. *Sargasso*, the ballet for ABT, was a technical and emotional role for Sallie Wilson, the principal dancer. It was far less for us, the small ensemble, but it was rewarding to dance nonetheless.

I rather hoped that *Sargasso* would be the last ballet I would dance before my retiring. It was not. It was as a housewife in *Billy the Kid*, choreography by Eugene Loring and a Ballet Theatre staple. This role was, perhaps, the least impressive and the most disliked of my career and it took place during a Ballet Theatre season at Lincoln Center's recently completed State Theater.

I sat in the dressing room applying my make-up, just as I had done hundreds of times before. As I completed each step I tossed the half full jars, tubes and bottles of make-up, and make-up remover into the basket by my side. The loud clanking sound each made as it hit the metal basket had a satisfying sound of finality. It fit my mood. I opened the hand painted, lacquered box that Bob had given me in Russia. I removed the rhinestone earrings that had given a finishing touch to the more theatrical roles in my career and admired their shine one last time. I gently dropped them into the basket. My thirteen-year career was over. I kept the box.

Having retired before Paul, I began teaching and he continued touring—never a good idea for a marriage. Before long, the eight-year marriage ended. I put it behind me. I put friendships with colleagues who were still performing behind me. I put my thirteen years with the Met Opera, The Joffrey, and ABT behind me. I put the years of work and hope that had preceded those years behind me. Years passed before I attended a ballet performance.

Even so, I taught and I became a teacher with dedication, enthusiasm, and skill. My life as a dancer, it seems, could not be erased. It colored every class I taught and by teaching I eventually began to appreciate my dancer's life and to recapture the memories I now cherish.

I began annual visits to see the Joffrey Ballet at the New York City Center Theater. As much as I enjoyed seeing the company, the highlight of the trip was always exchanging a few words with Bob.

At the far end of the hallway alongside the City Center stage, there was a door that led backstage. Before and after intermissions, I looked for Bob to either hurry into the house or rush backstage immediately after a ballet was over.

These meetings were short, but warm. Company talk filled our few minutes together. The conversations never seemed to come to a close; they simply ended.

Our encounters began with Bob's face lighting up upon seeing me. I don't think we exchanged ritual pecks on the cheek. Bob asked my opinions of the company's new ballets. Teaching young teenage dancers and beginning adults in Boston and reading monthly issues of *Dance Magazine* insured insights that were neither knowledgeable nor up to date, but Bob did not ask for my opinions for his edification. I think he was just curious about what others (including me) thought.

Company party for American Ballet Theatre in Bogota, Columbia. (Left to right) Lucia Chase, the author, Edward Verso, Gretchen Schumacher, and Rosalin Ricci. 1964. (From the collection of Marie Paquet-Nesson)

Wisely, he seemed to follow his own counsel. However, I was not shy about expressing my personal views, all of which I believed to be unerringly valuable. Bob's response was always the same: little or none.

Another former dancer, a musician, a fan, a friend, or a friend of a friend or two would soon be congregating at a shoulder's width behind us. Listening with a smile both expectant and reticent, they waited for their turn to speak but Bob was impatient to take his seat, get backstage, or just cease talking. Turning to the reverential gathering and me, he would say, "Do you know one another?" Without waiting for an answer, he introduced us to one another and when all eyes were redirected away from him, he was gone. In a flash, the conversation was over. It hardly mattered. I was exuberantly happy. I felt connected to Bob. The New York visit was perfect.

Bob always watched all the performances and he critiqued every minute. From past experience I knew that, during intermissions, he would never say anything to his dancers that might have distracted them from the rest of the program. But his darting, eagle-like eyes and prodigious memory would have seen and remembered details that would pour into the next day's rehearsals. And, perhaps, there would be someone who would have earned a compliment that, if as infrequent as I remembered, would never be forgotten.

Over the years Bob changed from looking young, like a traditional college student, to a man with physical substance and graying beard, more like a college professor. It gave Bob great satisfaction to know that his company had become an important American company. He liked knowing that his retired dancers remained a part of the dance world. Some had gone on to direct companies, choreograph, and, for many of us, teach. Former company members were on the Joffrey Ballet staff or the faculty of the Joffrey School.

I believe that Bob's hope was to see the Joffrey Ballet become a secure link in the lineage of dance history.

"Don't stop teaching," he said to me during our last telephone conversation. "Keep your sense of humor," he added. He spoke from his hospital room. I was ecstatic to hear his voice sound so strong. Even though I knew that he had been ill for a long time, the thought of his not recovering was unbearable. The unbearable happened. Three weeks later, Robert Joffrey was gone.

Accompanying me to the memorial service, my mother felt no need to try to console me. She knew that she could not. It was enough that she was there beside me. She was with me when I took a rose from one of the floral arrangements.

Today, my closest friends are dancers with whom I have reconnected over the years. We rarely talk about the past, but we share it. What is the common thread that ties us together? Is it the excitement, the stage fright, the exultation, the sore muscles and lack of sleep, the harmony between us, the disharmony between us, the love of travel, the dislike of endless tours, the teachers and ballets we loved, the teachers and ballets we didn't? Yes, and more. Reigning supreme was the experience of being struck by Terpsichore, the Greek Muse of Dance, and it was this experience that is at the core of us all.

I remember hearing the phrase, "Beauty's sweetly lingering ghost." It expresses perfectly the look in the eyes of those who speak of these illusive moments and no one has related this experience more simply or dramatically than Wakefield Poole, a corps de ballet dancer who had danced with Ballet Russe de Monte Carlo. Interviewed for the documentary film, *Ballets Russes*, he began reminiscing about being on stage during the second act in *Swan Lake*. "We men had nothing to do, just standing around," he began. His voice, mannered and flip, was that of a "Broadway Gypsy," a performer who, after years on the boards, sounds self-deprecating and cynical. Then, as he continued his voice lowered, "I was on stage and looked around. The swans in their white tutus were bathed in a blue haze and, suddenly, I thought, 'I am in a ballet company.' It was very moving." His face softened. "The audience was in total rapture. It was the most fulfilling time in the Ballet Russe." His eyes filled with tears. Ah, there it was! "Beauty's sweetly lingering ghost."

I believe my having been a swan in a white tutu and bathed in a blue haze, myself, enriched my teaching. I taught for twenty-five years, the last ten back in my hometown of Boston, first in my own studio and then at the Boston Ballet School. I attended and enjoyed many performances in Boston and in New York City. I enjoyed appreciating my past and was glad that my mother had saved old photographs, letters, and programs. I was happy, once again, to meet former colleagues.

And so, one day in February 2002, I was on my way to meet a friend, a former dancer with Ballet Theatre who was now director of a ballet company in the Midwest. I had not seen him since we danced at Lincoln Center's State Theater forty-five years earlier. He was in Boston to audition students for his company's summer program, one of many representatives from companies large and small, who made annual visits to recruit talented young dancers.

The Boston Ballet School had rented out its large company studio for the audition. Although hopeful dancers still go to New York for summer programs, many more choose—or their parents' choose—programs affiliated with companies all across the country.

Entering the elevator, I pushed the fifth floor button. The neon light, white walls, and clicking sounds that marked the assent reminded me of the elevators at the State Theater at Lincoln Center, elevators that took the dancers from the sub basement level dressing rooms up to the stage. Unlike the spiral steel staircases and dusky hallways in old theaters that led us gradually from the dressing rooms to the wings and the brilliantly lit stage, the neutral elevators at the State Theater seemed to suspend time. It made the flow towards the footlights much too abrupt.

The Boston Ballet elevator doors opened. Through the wide, window-wall of the studio I saw nervous teenage hopefuls warming up and practicing pirouettes. I stepped into the hallway where my friend was waiting. "Marie Paquet," he exclaimed with arms outstretched. A few hurried teasing questions about the passage of time followed before he laughed, "I'll never forget how you sauntered into the theater and did not even do a proper barre before going on stage. You were a riot." Answering with sarcasm, I sounded like the person I had become towards the end of my career. I wished I had not. He laughed again but I did not. I put the photos I had brought back in my bag. Another time, I thought. He went to work and I took the elevator down to the street.

I had planned to show off my students. The slim fourteen-year olds were in identical poses, one girl behind another. Everyone had placed one of her hands perfectly on the barre slightly bent and ten inches or so in front of their bodies. The other arm was rounded in front of their waists, elbows and wrists carefully held as to avoid sharp angles. No fingers stuck up or out or down. Legs were lifted directly to the side and arrow-like, feet pointed straight into the camera. Shoulders were down and upper backs were slightly arched, causing each young adolescent chest to lift into an impossible height, the proud stance of a ballerina. Their sweet faces focused beyond the camera into the gaze of some future audience. Their dedication was a testament to my own.

Being reminded of my "Broadway Gypsy" days had startled me. And why would it not? It had been over two decades since I had reconnected with memories of Terpsichore. And once remembered, her grace sat and continues to sit strongly in my soul. It is to Bob that I owe that grace.

Bob Joffrey's birthday present to me in 1963, the Russian paper mache box, still shines with black lacquer and dazzles with color. Since 1988, it has held a single dried rose, a rose from his memorial service.

I was left with another gift, a gift as precious as the grace of Terpsichore. Saying goodbye during our last conversation Bob said, "You have my love."

(photo credit: Erik Hanson)

Marie Paquet-Nesson's thirteen-year professional ballet career began with a three-week replacement job with the Radio City Music Hall Ballet Corps. She went on to dance with The Metropolitan Opera Ballet, The Robert Joffrey Ballet, and American Ballet Theatre. She taught for over twenty-five years in the Boston area and now resides in Cambridge, Massachusetts.